5D Mind

by

Eric M. Ndwiga

Double 9
BOOKS

5D Mind
by Eric M. Ndwiga

ISBN: 978-93-61157-80-6

Published by

DOUBLE 9 BOOKS
2/13-B, Ansari Road
Daryaganj, New Delhi – 110002
info@double9books.com
www.double9books.com
Tel. 011-40042856

ABOUT THE AUTHOR

Eric Mugendi Ndwiga is a leader in the new thought movement,after a bitter divorce that left him depressed and stuck he embarked on a journey to lmmerse himself in to his long-known personal growth materials to overcome depression and stagnation after acquiring vast knowledge and applying the various techniques and tools he overcame depression effortlessly and decided to write a series of personal growth books titled 5D MIND to equip people from all walks of life to overcome whatever life throws at them he believes this series of books should be taught in school and is working towards the fruition of the idea "The world needs not a broken doctor or a frustrated teacher it needs a 5d doctor to let the patient know healing comes from within or a 5d teacher to teach the student how to teach oneself " he often says.

CONTENTS

Chapter 6
Navigating the Dimensions

Chapter 7
Intuition and Inner Guidance

Chapter 8
The Power of Thought

Chapter 9
Embracing Change and Transformation

Chapter 10
Beyond Time and Space

Chapter 11
Healing and Balancing Energies

Chapter 12
Creating Your Reality

Chapter 13
Awakening the Inner Creative Genius

Chapter 14
The Dance of Synchronicity

Chapter 15
Embodying Unconditional Love

Chapter 16
Expanding Conscious Relationships

Chapter 17
The Unity of Body, Mind, and Spirit

Chapter 18
Multidimensional Perception of Time

Chapter 19
The Evolutionary Path

Chapter 20
Living as a 5D Being

Expanding Love's Horizons

Expanding Consciousness in the Digital Age

Chapter 1
Understanding the 5D Mind

Chapter 2
Cultivating a 5D Mindset

Chapter 3
Harnessing the Power of Intuition

Chapter 4
Creating Connection in a Digital World

Chapter 5
Expanding Consciousness Through Technology

Elevating Corporate Consciousness for Success in the Digital Age

Chapter 4

Chapter 5

Chapter 6

Chapter 7

UNLEASHED

Chapter 1
Introduction to the 5D Mind

Understanding the concept of the 5D Mind

In a world where we often perceive reality through the lens of three dimensions, the concept of the 5D Mind opens up a whole new realm of possibilities. It invites us to expand our understanding of existence beyond the confines of what is tangible and visible, and delve into the realms of higher consciousness. The 5D Mind represents a shift in perception, a recognition that there are dimensions beyond the physical, and that our minds have the capacity to access and explore these realms.

The term "5D" refers to the fifth dimension, which is not limited by time and space as we know it. It is a dimension where the boundaries dissolve, and interconnectedness becomes apparent. In the 5D Mind, we move beyond linear thinking and embrace a holistic perspective that encompasses the spiritual, emotional, mental, and energetic aspects of our being.

To understand the 5D Mind, it is essential to recognize that we are more than just physical bodies. We possess a consciousness that transcends the limitations of our physical existence. This consciousness is interconnected with the greater web of life, resonating with universal energy and wisdom.

In the 5D Mind, perception takes on a new meaning. It expands beyond the five senses, allowing us to tap into intuitive knowing, subtle energies, and higher guidance. We begin to recognize the power of our thoughts and beliefs in shaping our reality, and we learn to navigate the multidimensional landscape with mindfulness and intention.

The journey into the 5D Mind is a process of awakening, of becoming aware of the vast potential within us and the interconnectedness of all things. It is a journey that requires openness, curiosity, and a willingness to question the limitations of our current understanding.

Throughout this book, we will explore various facets of the 5D Mind and delve into practices and perspectives that can help us expand our consciousness. We will embark on a transformative journey, touching upon topics such as mindfulness, intuition, energy, manifestation, and the integration of body, mind, and spirit.

As we venture into the realm of the 5D Mind, it is important to approach it with an open heart and an open mind. This exploration may challenge our preconceived notions and stretch our understanding, but it also holds the potential to unlock profound insights and empower us to live more fulfilling and purposeful lives.

So, let us embark on this journey together, as we delve into the realms of the 5D Mind and awaken to the limitless possibilities that await us. Get ready to expand your perception, embrace your innate wisdom, and tap into the transformative power of the 5D Mind.

Exploring the dimensions beyond the physical realm

In the vast tapestry of existence, there exists a realm beyond the limitations of our physical reality. It is a dimension where consciousness expands, where time and space become malleable, and where the subtle threads of energy interweave to form a profound interconnectedness. Welcome to the realm of the 5D Mind.

As human beings, we often perceive the world through our five senses, experiencing the three-dimensional reality that surrounds us. We navigate through life, guided by what is tangible and measurable. However, there is a growing understanding that our existence encompasses more than what meets the eye.

The 5D Mind represents a shift in our awareness, an expansion beyond the boundaries of the physical realm. It invites us to explore dimensions that exist beyond the scope of our ordinary perception. These dimensions transcend the constraints of time and space, allowing us to glimpse the interconnectedness of all things.

When we begin to explore the dimensions beyond the physical realm, we open ourselves to a vast landscape of consciousness. We recognize that there is more to our existence than the material world. We become aware of subtle energies, intuitive knowing, and the power of our thoughts to shape our reality.

The exploration of these dimensions requires a willingness to let go of the limitations imposed by the three-dimensional thinking. It calls for an open mind, a sense of wonder, and a curiosity to delve into the mysteries that lie beyond the veil.

In the realm of the 5D Mind, we start to perceive reality as a multidimensional tapestry. We become aware that there are layers beyond the physical, where subtle energies dance and intertwine. These dimensions house realms of higher consciousness, where wisdom, creativity, and spiritual insights abound.

As we embark on this exploration, we encounter concepts such as astral planes, higher dimensions, and alternate realities. We learn that time is not linear but can be experienced simultaneously, and that space is not limited to physical distance but can be traversed through consciousness.

Exploring the dimensions beyond the physical realm requires a shift in our perception. It necessitates a letting go of rigid beliefs and an openness to the unknown. It is an invitation to expand our consciousness and to embrace the vastness of our being.

Throughout this book, we will delve deeper into the exploration of these dimensions beyond the physical realm. We will explore topics such as astral projection, lucid dreaming, meditation, energy work, and connecting with spiritual guides. Together, we will embark on a journey that will expand our understanding of existence and awaken us to the limitless possibilities that lie within the 5D Mind.

So, prepare yourself for an adventure beyond the confines of the physical world. Open your mind, open your heart, and step into the realm of the 5D Mind, where the dimensions beyond the physical realm await your exploration.

Chapter 2
Unleashing the Power of Perception

Expanding your perception beyond the limitations of the 3D world

In the realm of the 3D world, our perception is often confined to what is immediately tangible and visible. We rely on our five senses to navigate and understand the world around us. However, the 5D Mind invites us to go beyond these limitations and tap into a deeper, more expansive perception.

Perception is the lens through which we interpret and make sense of our reality. It shapes our beliefs, influences our thoughts and emotions, and ultimately molds our experiences. When we expand our perception, we open ourselves to a whole new range of possibilities and insights.

To unleash the power of perception, we must first recognize that there is more to reality than what we can perceive with our five senses alone. There are subtle energies, frequencies, and dimensions that interplay and coexist alongside the physical realm. By expanding our perception, we can begin to tune into these subtler aspects of existence.

Expanding our perception requires a shift in consciousness. It entails becoming aware of the filters and biases that color our understanding of the world. It involves questioning our assumptions, beliefs, and conditioned ways of seeing, and opening ourselves to new perspectives.

One way to expand perception is through mindfulness. By cultivating present-moment awareness, we can transcend the automatic patterns of thought and perception that often govern our experience. Mindfulness allows us to observe our thoughts and emotions without judgment, creating space for a broader, more objective perception.

Another powerful tool for expanding perception is meditation. Through regular meditation practice, we can quiet the mind, enhance our focus, and access deeper states of consciousness. In these altered states, we can tap into intuitive knowing, receive insights, and glimpse the interconnectedness of all things.

Intuition is a key aspect of expanded perception. It is the inner knowing that goes beyond logical reasoning. By honing our intuition, we can access information and guidance that transcends the limitations of the rational mind. Trusting our intuition allows us to navigate the complexities of life with greater clarity and wisdom.

Expanding perception also involves exploring the realms of energy and vibration. Everything in the universe is made up of energy, and by attuning ourselves to different frequencies, we can perceive subtle energies that are otherwise unseen. Practices such as energy healing, Reiki, and Qi Gong can help us develop this sensitivity to energy and expand our perception of the interconnected web of life.

As we expand our perception beyond the limitations of the 3D world, we begin to experience reality in a more holistic and multidimensional way. We start to recognize the influence of our thoughts, emotions, and energetic resonance on the world around us. We become co-creators, actively shaping our reality through conscious perception and intention.

In the journey of unleashing the power of perception, we invite you to explore various practices and perspectives that can help expand your awareness. Through mindfulness, meditation, intuition, and an understanding of energy, you can tap into the vast potential of perception and unlock new dimensions of consciousness.

So, open your mind and senses to the possibilities that lie beyond the confines of the 3D world. Embrace the power of perception and embark on a journey of expanded awareness. The realm of the 5D Mind awaits your exploration, offering a richer, more vibrant tapestry of existence.

Developing a heightened sense of awareness

In the realm of the 5D Mind, perception is not limited to the surface level of our experiences. It extends far beyond the ordinary senses, inviting us to develop a heightened sense of awareness that penetrates the depths of existence. By unleashing the power of perception and cultivating a heightened state of awareness, we can tap into the vast reservoirs of wisdom and insight that lie within us.

Developing a heightened sense of awareness starts with the practice of mindfulness. Mindfulness is the art of being fully present in the moment, observing our thoughts, emotions, and sensations with non-judgmental awareness. When we engage in mindfulness, we become attuned to the subtleties of our inner and outer experiences, opening ourselves to a deeper level of perception.

One way to cultivate mindfulness and heighten awareness is through conscious breathing. By bringing our attention to the breath, we anchor ourselves in the present moment, calming the mind and fostering a state of focused awareness. With each breath, we become more attuned to the sensations within our bodies, the movements of our thoughts, and the subtleties of our surroundings.

Another powerful practice for developing heightened awareness is meditation. Through regular meditation, we train the mind to become still and centered, allowing us to access deeper states of consciousness. In these states, we can observe the patterns of our thoughts, connect with our intuition, and expand our perception beyond the limitations of the physical world.

Expanding awareness also involves engaging our senses fully. Often, we go through life on autopilot, unaware of the richness of our sensory experiences. By consciously engaging with our senses—touch, taste, smell, sight, and hearing—we open ourselves to a world of vibrant sensations. We can savor the taste of food, feel the warmth of the sun on our skin, listen to the melody of nature, and see the intricate beauty in every moment.

Developing a heightened sense of awareness requires us to be fully present and engaged in the here and now. It means letting go of distractions and cultivating a deep connection with the present moment. By doing so, we can perceive the subtle nuances that often go unnoticed, gaining insight into ourselves, others, and the world around us.

As we develop heightened awareness, we also become more attuned to the energy that flows through and around us. Energy is the life force that animates all things, and by tuning into it, we can sense the underlying currents that shape our experiences. Practices such as Qigong, Tai Chi, and energy healing can help us develop sensitivity to energy and enhance our perception of the subtle realms.

In the journey of unleashing the power of perception and developing a heightened sense of awareness, patience and practice are key. It is a continual process of deepening our presence and expanding our perception. With each moment of conscious awareness, we awaken to the richness of life and the interconnectedness of all things.

So, embrace the power of awareness and embark on the path of heightened perception. Through mindfulness, meditation, engaging your senses, and attuning to energy, you can awaken a profound sense of connection and tap into the infinite wellspring of wisdom within you. The realm of the 5D Mind beckons, inviting you to explore the depths of perception and experience the world with heightened awareness.

Chapter 3
The Art of Mindfulness

Cultivating mindfulness in everyday life

In our fast-paced and often chaotic world, cultivating mindfulness has become a powerful antidote to the distractions and stresses that surround us. The art of mindfulness invites us to bring our attention fully to the present moment, to cultivate a deep sense of awareness, and to engage with life's experiences with openness and non-judgment.

Mindfulness is not just a practice reserved for formal meditation sessions. It is a way of being that can be integrated into every aspect of our lives. By cultivating mindfulness in everyday life, we can transform ordinary moments into opportunities for presence, insight, and profound connection.

One of the fundamental aspects of mindfulness is bringing our attention to the present moment. We often find ourselves caught up in regrets about the past or worries about the future, allowing these thoughts to dominate our experience. Mindfulness invites us to gently guide our awareness back to the here and now, where life unfolds in its fullest richness.

To cultivate mindfulness in everyday life, we can start by bringing our attention to our breath. The breath serves as an anchor, grounding us in the present moment. By noticing the sensation of each inhalation and exhalation, we connect with the rhythm of life and become more attuned to the present.

Another way to infuse mindfulness into everyday activities is by practicing conscious observation. Whether it's eating a meal, walking in nature, or engaging in a conversation, we can bring our full attention to the experience. We can savor the flavors and textures of food, feel the earth beneath our feet as we walk, and truly listen to the words and nuances in our conversations.

Mindfulness also involves non-judgmental awareness. It is the practice of observing our thoughts, emotions, and sensations without getting caught up in them or labeling them as good or bad. Through this non-judgmental awareness, we can cultivate a sense of inner peace and acceptance, allowing life to unfold as it is without resistance.

Practicing mindfulness in everyday life also includes self-compassion. It is about treating ourselves with kindness and understanding, especially during challenging moments. When we encounter difficulties or make mistakes, we can bring a gentle awareness to our inner experience and offer ourselves compassion and forgiveness.

In addition to individual practices, mindfulness can be cultivated through community and connection. Engaging in mindful conversations, deep listening, and acts of kindness can create an atmosphere of presence and mindfulness in our interactions with others. By being fully present with those around us, we nourish meaningful connections and foster a sense of unity.

As we cultivate mindfulness in everyday life, we begin to discover the transformative power of the present moment. We realize that the beauty and richness of life reside in the simple moments that often go unnoticed. By bringing a mindful presence to these moments, we awaken to the profound depth and interconnectedness of our existence.

So, embrace the art of mindfulness and make it a part of your daily life. Allow yourself to fully engage with the present moment, to observe your thoughts and emotions with non-judgmental awareness, and to connect deeply with others. Through the practice of mindfulness, you can transform ordinary moments into extraordinary opportunities for growth, connection, and joy.

Practicing Presence and Living in the Present Moment

In our modern world, it is easy to get caught up in the busyness and distractions that surround us. Our minds often wander between regrets of the past and worries about the future, leaving us disconnected from the richness of the present moment. However, by practicing presence and living in the present moment, we can reclaim our sense of aliveness and deepen our experience of life.

Presence is the art of being fully engaged and attentive to the here and now. It is a state of mind where our awareness is anchored in the present moment, free from the incessant chatter of the past and future. When we practice presence, we cultivate a deep sense of connection with ourselves, others, and the world around us.

One of the key elements of practicing presence is developing awareness of our thoughts and emotions. We often get carried away by the stream of thoughts that flow through our minds, taking us away from the present moment. By observing our thoughts with non-judgmental awareness, we can begin to detach from their pull and bring our attention back to the present.

A powerful tool for practicing presence is mindfulness meditation. This practice involves intentionally focusing our attention on the present moment, typically by observing the breath or bodily sensations. Through regular meditation, we train our minds to stay anchored in the present, cultivating a sense of calm and clarity that extends beyond the meditation cushion and into our everyday lives.

Another way to cultivate presence is by engaging our senses fully. Our senses are gateways to the present moment, offering us direct access to the richness of our sensory experiences. Whether it's savoring the flavors of a meal, feeling the touch of a loved one, or listening to the sounds of nature, we can immerse ourselves fully in the present through the senses.

Practicing presence also involves letting go of the need for constant doing and striving. We live in a culture that often values productivity and achievement above all else, causing us to overlook the simple joys of being.

By embracing the art of simply being, we create space to appreciate the beauty and wonder of each moment, free from the burden of constantly chasing after the next thing.

Living in the present moment also requires acceptance and non-resistance. We may encounter challenges, discomfort, or unwanted experiences, but by accepting them without resistance, we can reduce unnecessary suffering and find peace in the midst of difficulties. This acceptance allows us to fully engage with what is, rather than longing for what could have been or should be.

Practicing presence and living in the present moment is not about escaping from the past or ignoring future plans. It is about bringing a quality of awareness and aliveness to each moment, recognizing that the present is all we truly have. By living in the present, we deepen our connections, find joy in the ordinary, and unlock the fullness of life's experiences.

So, make a commitment to practice presence and embrace the gift of the present moment. Through mindfulness, meditation, engaging your senses, and cultivating acceptance, you can awaken to the richness and beauty that is available to you right here, right now. By living in the present moment, you open yourself to a world of wonder, gratitude, and profound connection with yourself and the world around you.

Chapter 4
Journey into Consciousness

Exploring the different levels of consciousness

Consciousness is the essence of our being, the very core of our existence. It is the foundation upon which our thoughts, emotions, and experiences unfold. As we embark on a journey into consciousness, we open ourselves to a vast realm of exploration and self-discovery.

At its most basic level, consciousness refers to our state of wakefulness and awareness of our surroundings. However, consciousness extends far beyond this surface level of perception. It encompasses various dimensions and levels that shape our understanding of ourselves and the world.

One way to explore consciousness is by delving into the levels of awareness. We can experience different states of consciousness, ranging from ordinary waking consciousness to deep meditative states, dream states, and even altered states induced by substances or spiritual practices.

Ordinary waking consciousness is the state in which we typically operate in our daily lives. It involves being aware of our thoughts, emotions, and the external environment. In this state, our consciousness is focused on the physical world and the immediate experiences we encounter.

As we deepen our exploration, we encounter altered states of consciousness. These states can be accessed through practices such as meditation, breathwork, or shamanic journeying. Altered states can bring us beyond the ordinary limitations of our everyday awareness, opening the door to expanded dimensions of consciousness.

Meditation, in particular, allows us to transcend the boundaries of ordinary waking consciousness and enter states of heightened awareness and inner stillness. Through meditation, we can access deeper layers of consciousness and tap into the infinite wellspring of wisdom and insight that resides within.

Dream states offer another gateway to exploring consciousness. In our dreams, we enter a realm where the boundaries of time, space, and physical laws dissolve. Dreams can provide profound insights, symbols, and messages that offer glimpses into the depths of our subconscious mind and the interconnectedness of all things.

Beyond altered states, we also encounter different levels of consciousness in our daily lives. These levels range from ordinary ego-based consciousness to transpersonal or spiritual consciousness. Each level offers a unique perspective and understanding of reality.

Ego-based consciousness is rooted in our individual identities and the narratives we construct about ourselves. It is the level of consciousness that emphasizes separation and the pursuit of personal desires and achievements. As we move beyond ego-based consciousness, we can access transpersonal levels that encompass a broader sense of unity, interconnectedness, and spiritual awareness.

Exploring consciousness also involves unraveling the layers of conditioning, beliefs, and patterns that shape our perception of reality. As we become aware of these influences, we can begin to free ourselves from their limitations and open up to new possibilities of perception and experience.

The journey into consciousness is a deeply personal and transformative one. It requires a willingness to question our assumptions, venture into the unknown, and embrace the mysteries of our own being. It is an invitation to connect with our true nature and explore the vast realms of existence that lie within and beyond.

As you embark on this journey into consciousness, embrace curiosity, open- mindedness, and a spirit of exploration. Allow yourself to delve into altered states, meditative practices, dream analysis, and self-reflection. By doing so, you can deepen your understanding of yourself, expand your perception of reality, and unlock the profound depths of consciousness that reside within you.

So, embark on this transformative journey into consciousness, and let your exploration guide you to new levels of awareness, insight, and self-realization. Through this exploration, you can awaken to the expansive nature of consciousness and uncover the timeless wisdom that lies at the heart of your being.

Awakening to your true nature and purpose

In our quest to understand the nature of consciousness, we inevitably embark on a journey of self-discovery. This journey takes us deep within ourselves, where we uncover the essence of our being and the purpose that calls us forward. It is a transformative expedition that leads us to awaken to our true nature and align with our unique purpose in life.

Awakening to our true nature begins with a recognition that we are more than just our physical bodies and thoughts. We are spiritual beings having a human experience, and consciousness is the thread that connects us to the vast web of existence. As we delve into this journey, we peel away the layers of conditioning, societal expectations, and limiting beliefs, revealing the radiant truth of who we really are.

This awakening often involves questioning our assumptions and beliefs about ourselves and the world. It requires a willingness to step outside the comfort zones of our familiar identities and explore the boundless possibilities that lie beyond. Through self-reflection, contemplation, and introspection, we gain insight into our core values, passions, and deepest desires.

As we awaken to our true nature, we also become attuned to the whispers of our soul. The soul is the essence of our being, the divine spark that resides within us. It holds the wisdom and guidance that aligns us with our life's purpose. By listening to the yearnings of our soul and following its guidance, we embark on a path that is uniquely ours, one that brings fulfillment, meaning, and contribution to the world.

To awaken to our purpose, we must cultivate presence and mindfulness. By staying fully engaged in the present moment, we create space for clarity and inspiration to arise. We begin to notice the synchronicities, the subtle nudges, and the signs that guide us along our path. This presence allows us to recognize and seize opportunities that align with our purpose, and to take inspired action that brings our unique gifts into the world.

The journey into consciousness and awakening to our true nature is not always smooth or linear. It may involve facing and healing past wounds, embracing our shadow aspects, and navigating the uncertainties of transformation. It requires courage, resilience, and self-compassion as we navigate the twists and turns of self-discovery.

Along this journey, it is essential to seek support and guidance. Engaging in spiritual practices, connecting with like-minded individuals, and seeking the wisdom of teachers and mentors can provide invaluable insights and encouragement. Surrounding ourselves with a supportive community can uplift and inspire us on our path of awakening.

As we awaken to our true nature and purpose, we not only experience personal transformation but also contribute to the collective evolution of consciousness. By embodying our authentic selves, we inspire others to do the same. Our aligned actions ripple out into the world, creating a positive impact and fostering a more conscious and harmonious society.

So, embrace the journey into consciousness and the awakening to your true nature and purpose. Dive deep into self-reflection, explore your passions, and listen to the whispers of your soul. Through presence, self-discovery, and alignment with your purpose, you can navigate the profound landscape of consciousness and embark on a transformative journey of personal and collective evolution.

Chapter 5
Connecting with Universal Energy

Understanding the interconnectedness of all things

In our journey into the depths of consciousness, we come to realize that we are not isolated beings, but integral parts of a vast and interconnected web of existence. At the heart of this interconnection lies universal energy — the life force that animates all things. In this chapter, we explore the significance of connecting with universal energy and understanding the profound interconnectedness that permeates the fabric of our reality.

Universal energy, also known as cosmic or divine energy, flows through every atom, molecule, and living being in the universe. It is the essence that connects us to each other, to nature, and to the larger cosmos. When we tap into this universal energy, we awaken to a profound sense of unity and oneness.

To connect with universal energy, we must first recognize that everything in the universe is made up of energy. Energy is not confined to physical forms but exists in a myriad of subtle vibrations and frequencies. By cultivating awareness and sensitivity to this energy, we can begin to experience its presence and influence in our lives.

One way to connect with universal energy is through mindfulness and presence. By slowing down, quieting the mind, and being fully present, we create space to perceive the subtle energetic currents that surround us. Through this awareness, we can begin to sense the interconnectedness of all things, realizing that we are an integral part of a vast energetic tapestry.

Another powerful way to connect with universal energy is through practices such as meditation, yoga, and breathwork. These practices allow us to enter a state of deep relaxation and inner stillness, where we become receptive to the subtle energetic flow. In these moments of connection, we can experience a sense of expansion, peace, and oneness with the universe.

Nature also provides a profound opportunity to connect with universal energy. By immersing ourselves in the natural world, we can attune ourselves to the rhythms and energies of the earth, plants, animals, and elements. Through this connection, we recognize that we are intimately interconnected with the entire ecosystem and that our well-being is intricately linked to the well-being of the planet.

Intention and visualization are powerful tools for connecting with universal energy. By setting clear intentions and visualizing the energy flowing through us, we can consciously direct and align our energy with the greater universal flow. This conscious engagement with universal energy empowers us to co-create our reality and manifest our desires with greater clarity and purpose.

In the exploration of universal energy, we must also acknowledge the role of intuition. Intuition is the innate wisdom that arises from our connection with universal energy. By quieting the noise of the mind and tuning into our intuitive guidance, we can access profound insights, inner knowing, and a deeper understanding of our place within the interconnected web of existence.

By connecting with universal energy, we begin to realize that we are not separate entities but interconnected threads woven into the tapestry of life. We understand that our thoughts, emotions, and actions have an impact not only on ourselves but also on the collective consciousness. This awareness brings a sense of responsibility, compassion, and reverence for all beings and the environment in which we exist.

So, embrace the journey of connecting with universal energy and exploring the profound interconnectedness of all things. Through mindfulness, practices such as meditation and breathwork, connecting with nature, setting intentions, and following your intuition, you can cultivate a deep and meaningful connection with universal energy. As you tap into this vast cosmic flow, you awaken to your role as a co-creator in the grand symphony of existence, bringing greater harmony, love, and purpose into your life and the world around you.

Harnessing the power of universal energy for personal transformation

In our exploration of consciousness and interconnectedness, we encounter the immense power of universal energy—a force that flows through all things and holds the potential for profound personal transformation. This chapter delves into the significance of connecting with universal energy and how we can harness its power to facilitate our own growth and evolution.

Universal energy, also known as divine energy or life force, is the animating power that permeates the universe. It is the source from which all life emerges and the energetic fabric that interconnects everything. By consciously connecting with this universal energy, we open ourselves to its transformative potential and align ourselves with the natural rhythms of existence.

Connecting with universal energy starts with cultivating a deep sense of presence and awareness. By quieting the mind, releasing distractions, and being fully present in the current moment, we create a receptive space for the flow of energy to enter our being. In this state of heightened awareness, we can begin to tap into the vast reservoirs of universal energy.

Meditation serves as a powerful gateway to connecting with universal energy. Through meditation, we enter a state of inner stillness and heightened consciousness, allowing us to attune ourselves to the subtle vibrations of the energy around and within us. With regular practice, meditation deepens our connection with universal energy, fostering personal transformation and spiritual growth.

Breathwork is another transformative practice that enables us to connect with universal energy. By consciously directing our breath, we infuse our bodies with revitalizing energy and create a harmonious flow within. Through specific breathwork techniques, we can activate and circulate this universal energy, facilitating healing, self-discovery, and personal transformation.

Intentions and affirmations play a crucial role in harnessing the power of universal energy. By setting clear and positive intentions, we focus our awareness and direct the flow of energy towards specific desired outcomes. Affirmations, when repeated with conviction, help reprogram our subconscious mind and align our energy with our intentions, enhancing the manifestation process.

Visualization serves as a potent tool for connecting with and harnessing universal energy. By creating vivid mental images and immersing ourselves in the sensory experience of achieving our desired outcomes, we align our thoughts and emotions with the energy frequency of manifestation. Visualization allows us to tap into the creative power of universal energy and accelerate our personal transformation.

When we consciously connect with universal energy, we invite healing and growth on all levels—physical, emotional, mental, and spiritual. This energy facilitates the release of stagnant patterns, limiting beliefs, and emotional blockages that hinder our progress. As we allow universal energy to flow through us, we experience a profound shift in our consciousness, fostering inner peace, clarity, and an expanded sense of self.

As we harness the power of universal energy for personal transformation, it is crucial to nurture a sense of gratitude and reverence. Expressing gratitude for the abundant energy available to us and the transformative experiences it facilitates enhances our connection with this universal force. By cultivating reverence for the interconnectedness of all life and the role we play in this grand tapestry, we deepen our alignment with universal energy.

So, embrace the journey of connecting with universal energy and tap into its transformative power. Through practices such as meditation, breathwork, intention setting, affirmations, and visualization, you can forge a deep and intimate relationship with universal energy. As you harness its power for personal transformation, you embark on a path of self-discovery, healing, and growth, aligning yourself with the natural flow of the universe and awakening to your fullest potential.

Chapter 6
Navigating the Dimensions

Delving into the realms of higher dimensions

In our exploration of consciousness and universal energy, we begin to realize that the reality we perceive is not limited to the three dimensions of space and one dimension of time. There are higher dimensions that exist beyond our ordinary perception, realms that hold immense wisdom, possibilities, and expanded states of being. In this chapter, we embark on a journey of navigating these dimensions and opening ourselves to the vastness of existence.

Dimensions are not physical places, but rather different levels of consciousness and energy that coexist with our familiar reality. They offer unique perspectives, expanded understanding, and access to realms beyond the limitations of the physical world. As we delve into the exploration of dimensions, we broaden our perception and tap into the boundless potential of existence.

The fourth dimension is often referred to as the dimension of time. It represents a fluid and ever-changing aspect of reality, where past, present, and future intertwine. As we navigate the fourth dimension, we gain insights into the patterns, cycles, and interconnectedness of events in our lives. It allows us to transcend linear time and access a more holistic understanding of our experiences.

Beyond the fourth dimension lies the fifth dimension, often associated with higher states of consciousness and spiritual awareness. In the fifth dimension, the limitations of space and time dissolve, and we experience a sense of unity and interconnectivity with all beings and the universe. It is a realm where thoughts, intentions, and emotions have a profound impact on shaping our reality. Navigating the fifth dimension requires an open heart, expanded awareness, and a deep resonance with love and compassion.

The exploration of dimensions also includes the possibility of accessing parallel realities or alternate dimensions. These are realms that exist alongside our familiar reality, each with its own unique set of circumstances and possibilities. By delving into the concept of parallel realities, we open ourselves to the idea that multiple versions of ourselves and our experiences coexist simultaneously, offering infinite potentials and choices.

To navigate the dimensions, it is crucial to cultivate heightened awareness and develop the ability to discern subtle energies and frequencies. Practices such as meditation, mindfulness, and energy work help us refine our perception and attune ourselves to the subtle vibrations of these higher realms. Through these practices, we can access higher states of consciousness and connect with the wisdom and guidance that emanate from the dimensions beyond.

It is important to approach the exploration of dimensions with an open mind, curiosity, and discernment. As we navigate these realms, we may encounter experiences that challenge our existing beliefs and expand our understanding of reality. It is essential to integrate these experiences with groundedness and discernment, always seeking to align with our inner truth and highest good.

The journey of navigating dimensions is a deeply personal and transformative one. It invites us to go beyond the boundaries of our familiar reality and embrace the infinite possibilities that exist within the vastness of existence. It is a journey of self-discovery, spiritual growth, and the expansion of consciousness.

As we navigate the dimensions, we gain a broader perspective of our place in the universe and our interconnectedness with all beings. We tap into our innate creative potential and co-create our reality in alignment with higher states of consciousness. This exploration guides us to embrace our multidimensional nature and live a more purposeful, joyful, and expansive life.

So, embark on the journey of navigating the dimensions. Through mindfulness, meditation, energy work, and a deep resonance with love and compassion, you can expand your perception and connect with the realms of higher consciousness. As you navigate these dimensions, you open yourself to the wisdom, possibilities, and transformative experiences that await, and you embody the fullness of your multidimensional nature.

Learning to navigate and utilize their inherent wisdom

As we delve into the exploration of dimensions, we discover vast realms of consciousness and energy that hold profound wisdom and transformative potential. In this chapter, we embark on a journey of learning to navigate these dimensions and harness their inherent wisdom for our personal growth, spiritual evolution, and co-creation of reality.

Navigating the dimensions requires developing a heightened sense of awareness and attunement to subtle energies. Through meditation, mindfulness, and energetic practices, we refine our perception and expand our consciousness to connect with the multidimensional aspects of existence. By cultivating presence and deepening our intuition, we can navigate these realms with clarity and discernment.

Each dimension offers its own unique wisdom and insights. As we explore these realms, it is crucial to approach them with an open mind and a willingness to receive the teachings they have to offer. The wisdom of the dimensions transcends conventional knowledge and invites us to embrace new perspectives and expanded understandings of reality.

The fourth dimension, often associated with time, holds the wisdom of cycles, patterns, and the interconnectedness of events. Navigating the fourth dimension allows us to gain a broader perspective of our experiences, seeing beyond linear time and understanding the deeper meaning and purpose behind the events in our lives. It provides an opportunity to heal past wounds, release old patterns, and create new possibilities for the future.

In the fifth dimension, we tap into the wisdom of unity, interconnectivity, and higher states of consciousness. This realm invites us to transcend the limitations of the ego and embrace love, compassion, and oneness as guiding principles in our lives. Navigating the fifth dimension empowers us to co- create our reality from a place of expanded awareness, aligning our thoughts, emotions, and actions with the highest good of all.

As we navigate the dimensions, we may encounter parallel realities— alternate versions of ourselves and different possibilities that exist alongside our current reality. Exploring these parallel realities allows us to expand our sense of what is possible and make conscious choices that align with our deepest desires and soul's purpose. It reminds us that we are not bound by a single path, but have the power to shape our experiences and co-create our reality.

To effectively utilize the inherent wisdom of the dimensions, we must integrate these experiences into our daily lives. It is not enough to simply explore these realms in meditation or during moments of heightened awareness. We must bring the insights and wisdom gained from these journeys into practical application, incorporating them into our thoughts, beliefs, choices, and actions.

Practices such as journaling, self-reflection, and intention setting are powerful tools for integrating the wisdom of the dimensions. By writing about our experiences, reflecting on the insights gained, and setting clear intentions, we anchor the wisdom into our conscious awareness and manifest it in our lives. Regular contemplation and integration deepen our understanding and enable us to embody the wisdom we have acquired.

As we navigate the dimensions and utilize their inherent wisdom, we embark on a transformative journey of personal and spiritual growth. We awaken to the vastness of our own potential and the interconnectedness of all beings and aspects of existence. The wisdom gained from these explorations becomes a guiding light, illuminating our path and empowering us to create lives filled with purpose, joy, and alignment with our soul's calling.

So, embrace the journey of navigating the dimensions. Cultivate awareness, deepen your intuition, and explore the wisdom of the fourth and fifth dimensions. Embrace the possibilities of parallel realities and integrate the insights gained into your daily life. As you navigate these realms and utilize their inherent wisdom, you embark on a path of self-discovery, transformation, and conscious co-creation with the expansive and multidimensional nature of existence.

Chapter 7
Intuition and Inner Guidance

Honing your intuitive abilities

Intuition is a powerful and innate faculty that resides within each of us. It is the language of the soul, the guiding compass that leads us towards our highest potential and aligns us with the wisdom of the universe. In this chapter, we explore the significance of intuition and delve into practices for honing our intuitive abilities.

Intuition is often described as a deep knowing, a gut feeling, or an inner voice that speaks to us beyond logical reasoning. It is the subtle whisper that nudges us in a certain direction, alerts us to potential opportunities or challenges, and provides insights that surpass the limitations of our conscious mind. By honing our intuitive abilities, we tap into a wellspring of wisdom that can guide us through all aspects of life.

To cultivate and strengthen our intuition, it is essential to create space for silence and stillness. In the midst of the busyness of daily life, we can easily become disconnected from our intuitive guidance. By incorporating practices such as meditation, nature walks, or journaling into our routine, we create moments of quietude where we can listen to the whispers of our inner guidance.

Trusting our intuition requires developing a deep sense of self-trust and self- awareness. It involves recognizing and honoring the signals and sensations that arise within us. Pay attention to your body's responses, such as sensations in the gut or tingling sensations. These physical cues often accompany intuitive insights and can serve as signposts along our path.

Journaling is a valuable tool for connecting with our intuition. By writing freely and without judgment, we create a space to channel our inner wisdom onto the page. Through journaling, we can explore our thoughts, feelings, and insights, uncovering hidden patterns and gaining clarity on our intuitive guidance. Regularly reviewing our journal entries helps us discern the recurring themes and messages that emerge from our intuition.

Dreams offer a gateway to the realm of intuition and symbolism. Keep a dream journal by your bedside and record your dreams upon awakening. Dreams often contain valuable messages and insights from our subconscious mind and the universal wisdom. By paying attention to the symbols, emotions, and narratives within our dreams, we can access profound guidance and uncover hidden aspects of ourselves.

Another practice for honing intuition is developing our ability to listen deeply. This involves active and empathetic listening in our interactions with others. By truly hearing and understanding the perspectives and emotions of those around us, we cultivate a heightened sensitivity and receptivity to the subtle nuances of communication. This skill extends to listening to our own inner voice, allowing us to discern the guidance that arises from within.

Cultivating mindfulness and present-moment awareness is instrumental in honing our intuitive abilities. By being fully present, we attune ourselves to the subtleties of our experiences, enabling us to recognize the intuitive nudges and insights that arise. Engaging in mindfulness practices, such as conscious breathing or body scans, helps anchor us in the present and opens us to the wisdom of our intuition.

As we hone our intuitive abilities, it is important to release attachments to specific outcomes or expectations. Intuition often operates beyond the realm of logical understanding and may guide us towards unexpected paths. Trusting the process and surrendering to the flow of guidance allows us to embrace the wisdom and opportunities that our intuition presents.

Honing our intuitive abilities is an ongoing practice that requires patience, openness, and self-compassion. It is a journey of self-discovery and deepening connection with our inner wisdom. By embracing our intuitive gifts and integrating them into our lives, we empower ourselves to make decisions aligned with our authentic selves and to navigate life's challenges with grace and clarity.

So, honor the gift of intuition within you. Create space for silence and stillness, trust your inner guidance, and engage in practices such as journaling, dream exploration, active listening, and mindfulness. By honing your intuitive abilities, you awaken to a deeper understanding of yourself and the world, and you navigate life with greater clarity, purpose, and alignment with your soul's calling.

Trusting your inner guidance
for decision-making

In a world filled with external influences and endless options, we often find ourselves seeking guidance and clarity when making important decisions. However, deep within us lies a wellspring of wisdom—our intuition and inner guidance. In this chapter, we explore the significance of trusting our inner guidance and how it can serve as a reliable compass for decision- making.

Our intuition is a profound source of wisdom that arises from the depths of our being. It is a subtle and intuitive knowing that transcends rational thinking and taps into a deeper level of understanding. When we trust our inner guidance, we access a powerful tool for navigating life's choices and aligning ourselves with our highest good.

Trusting our inner guidance begins with developing self-awareness and cultivating a deep sense of inner stillness. In the midst of the noise and distractions of daily life, it can be challenging to hear the whispers of our intuition. By incorporating practices such as meditation, mindfulness, or moments of solitude, we create space for our inner wisdom to emerge.

When faced with decisions, it is essential to tune in and listen to the signals from within. Our intuition often communicates through subtle sensations, emotions, or a deep sense of knowing. Pay attention to the physical sensations in your body—tightness, expansion, or a sense of ease. Trusting our inner guidance requires attuning ourselves to these signals and allowing them to guide our decision-making process.

Journaling serves as a valuable tool for connecting with our inner guidance. By writing down our thoughts, feelings, and insights, we can tap into the deeper layers of our intuition. Engage in a stream-of-consciousness writing practice, allowing your intuition to guide the flow of words onto the page. Regularly reviewing your journal entries can unveil patterns and themes that provide valuable guidance for decision-making.

Dreams also offer a window into our subconscious mind and can provide profound insights for decision-making. Keep a dream journal by your bedside and record your dreams upon awakening. Reflect on the symbols, emotions, and narratives within your dreams, as they often hold messages from your intuition. By paying attention to your dreams, you can access hidden layers of wisdom that can inform your decision-making process.

Trusting our inner guidance requires embracing uncertainty and surrendering to the process. Our intuition may guide us towards paths that challenge our comfort zones or defy logic. It may not always offer immediate clarity or guarantee specific outcomes. However, by trusting the process and having faith in our inner wisdom, we open ourselves to opportunities and possibilities beyond what the rational mind can conceive.

It is important to discern the difference between our intuition and the voice of fear or ego. Fear-based thoughts often arise from a place of limitation and self-doubt, while intuition emerges from a place of expansiveness and alignment with our highest good. Cultivate self-awareness to distinguish between the two and trust the voice that resonates with authenticity, love, and compassion.

Practicing self-compassion is essential when trusting our inner guidance. We may make mistakes or encounter challenges along the way, but self- compassion allows us to embrace our imperfections and learn from our experiences. It reminds us that we are on a journey of growth and that our intuition is a trusted ally that supports our evolution.

By trusting our inner guidance for decision-making, we align ourselves with the wisdom of the universe and honor our authentic selves. It empowers us to make choices that are in harmony with our values, passions, and life purpose. As we trust our inner guidance, we step into a space of empowerment, clarity, and alignment with our highest potential.

So, cultivate trust in your inner guidance. Create moments of stillness, listen to the subtle signals within, and engage in practices such as journaling and dream exploration. Embrace uncertainty, discern the voice of fear from intuition, and practice self-compassion throughout the decision-making process. By trusting your inner guidance, you navigate life's choices with grace, wisdom, and alignment with your true self.

Chapter 8
The Power of Thought

Understanding the influence of thoughts on reality

Our thoughts are not mere fleeting mental processes; they hold an incredible power to shape our reality. In this chapter, we delve into the profound influence of thoughts and explore how they can create our experiences, shape our perception, and manifest our desires.

Thoughts serve as the building blocks of our reality. They are the seeds from which our experiences and actions emerge. Every thought we have carries a unique vibrational frequency that interacts with the energetic fabric of the universe. As we understand and harness the power of our thoughts, we unlock the potential to create a life filled with purpose, joy, and abundance.

The influence of thoughts begins with our perception of the world. Our thoughts shape the lens through which we view reality, filtering and interpreting our experiences. When we hold positive and empowering thoughts, our perception becomes attuned to opportunities, growth, and gratitude. Conversely, negative and limiting thoughts cloud our perception, distorting our experiences and reinforcing patterns of lack and struggle.

The power of thought extends beyond perception to the realm of manifestation. Our thoughts, when held consistently and with intention, have the capacity to manifest our desires into reality. The energy we invest in our thoughts aligns with similar energies in the universe, attracting corresponding experiences and circumstances. By consciously directing our thoughts, we become deliberate creators of our lives.

To harness the power of thought, it is essential to cultivate self-awareness and monitor the quality of our thoughts. Notice the patterns and tendencies that arise in your thinking—whether they are empowering or self-limiting. Awareness enables us to consciously shift our thoughts towards more positive, empowering, and abundant perspectives.

Affirmations play a pivotal role in reshaping our thought patterns. By consciously choosing positive and empowering statements and repeating them regularly, we rewire our subconscious mind and align our thoughts with our desires. Affirmations help us counteract self-limiting beliefs, instill new empowering beliefs, and set the stage for positive manifestations.

Visualizations serve as a powerful tool for harnessing the power of thought. By creating vivid mental images of our desired outcomes, we engage our imagination and emotions, aligning them with the frequency of our aspirations. Visualizations strengthen the neural pathways associated with our desired experiences, making them more accessible and likely to manifest.

Gratitude is a transformative practice that amplifies the power of thought. When we consciously cultivate gratitude, we shift our focus to the blessings and abundance already present in our lives. This shift in perspective not only attracts more positive experiences but also enhances our overall well-being and contentment. Gratitude aligns our thoughts with the energy of abundance, opening the floodgates for more to flow into our lives.

The power of thought is not limited to our personal experiences—it also extends to the collective consciousness. As we hold positive and loving thoughts, we contribute to a collective energy that uplifts and inspires. Our thoughts ripple out into the world, influencing the thoughts and experiences of others. By cultivating thoughts of compassion, unity, and harmony, we actively participate in the co-creation of a more loving and peaceful world.

Understanding the power of thought brings a sense of responsibility and empowerment. We have the ability to shape our reality by consciously choosing our thoughts and focusing our energy. By embracing positive, empowering, and abundant thoughts, we align ourselves with the infinite possibilities and potential that exist within and around us.

So, recognize the immense power of your thoughts. Cultivate self-awareness, monitor your thought patterns, and consciously choose thoughts that empower and uplift you. Engage in affirmations, visualizations, and gratitude practices to align your thoughts with your desires. As you harness the power of thought, you become a deliberate creator of your reality, shaping a life of purpose, joy, and abundance.

Harnessing the power of positive thinking

Our thoughts have the remarkable ability to shape our reality and influence the quality of our lives. In this chapter, we explore the transformative potential of positive thinking and how it can empower us to create a more fulfilling and joyful existence.

Positive thinking is more than simply maintaining a cheerful demeanor or ignoring challenges. It is a mindset that focuses on the constructive aspects of life, seeks opportunities for growth, and embraces an optimistic outlook. By harnessing the power of positive thinking, we can transform our thoughts, emotions, and actions to align with our highest potential.

The first step in harnessing the power of positive thinking is cultivating self-awareness. Notice the thoughts that arise in your mind—their quality, tone, and impact on your emotions and overall well-being. Awareness allows you to identify any patterns of negative thinking or self-limiting beliefs that may be holding you back. By shining a light on these patterns, you can consciously choose to replace them with positive and empowering thoughts.

Affirmations are powerful tools for reprogramming the mind with positive thoughts and beliefs. By intentionally choosing affirmations that align with your desired reality and repeating them regularly, you anchor positive and empowering thoughts in your subconscious mind. Affirmations help counteract self-doubt, cultivate self-confidence, and foster a mindset of abundance and possibility.

Gratitude is a cornerstone of positive thinking. By cultivating an attitude of gratitude, you shift your focus to the blessings and abundance present in your life. Acknowledging and appreciating the positive aspects of your experiences cultivates a sense of joy, contentment, and optimism. Gratitude amplifies positive thinking, attracting more reasons to be grateful and creating a virtuous cycle of positivity.

Visualization is a powerful technique that engages the power of positive thinking. By vividly imagining and visualizing your desired outcomes, you stimulate the mind's creative faculties and align your thoughts with the energy of manifestation. Visualization enhances your belief in the possibility of your dreams and motivates you to take inspired action towards their realization.

Surrounding yourself with positive influences is vital for sustaining a positive mindset. Choose to spend time with individuals who uplift and inspire you, engage in activities that bring you joy and fulfillment, and consume media and information that nourish your mind and soul. By consciously curating your environment, you create a supportive space that reinforces positive thinking and empowers you to thrive.

Challenges and setbacks are inevitable in life, but positive thinking allows you to reframe them as opportunities for growth and learning. Embrace a mindset of resilience and see challenges as stepping stones on your journey rather than insurmountable obstacles. By focusing on solutions and adopting a positive perspective, you can navigate through challenges with grace and emerge stronger than ever.

It is important to remember that positive thinking does not mean denying or suppressing negative emotions. Instead, it involves acknowledging and processing those emotions while consciously choosing to shift your thoughts towards more positive and empowering ones. Positive thinking is a tool for cultivating resilience, optimism, and a sense of empowerment in the face of life's ups and downs.

By harnessing the power of positive thinking, you create a powerful foundation for personal growth and transformation. Your thoughts shape your emotions, beliefs, and actions, influencing the outcomes and experiences you attract into your life. As you align your thoughts with positivity, you open yourself to a world of possibilities, cultivate meaningful relationships, and create a life that reflects your deepest desires and aspirations.

So, embrace the power of positive thinking. Cultivate self-awareness, practice affirmations, cultivate gratitude, visualize your dreams, and curate a supportive environment. See challenges as opportunities for growth and approach life with optimism and resilience. As you harness the power of positive thinking, you empower yourself to live a life filled with joy, abundance, and fulfillment.

Chapter 9
Embracing Change and Transformation

Embracing the fluidity of life

Change is an inherent and constant aspect of life. It sweeps through our experiences, relationships, and circumstances, inviting us to adapt, grow, and transform. In this chapter, we explore the significance of embracing change and the transformative power it holds for our personal growth and evolution.

Change is often met with resistance, as it disrupts our sense of familiarity and comfort. However, when we resist change, we deny ourselves the opportunity for growth and expansion. By embracing change, we open ourselves to new possibilities, experiences, and perspectives that can lead to profound transformation.

One of the keys to embracing change is cultivating a mindset of openness and flexibility. Instead of clinging to rigid expectations or attachments, we learn to flow with the natural rhythms of life. By releasing the need for control and surrendering to the fluidity of existence, we navigate change with grace and resilience.

Self-awareness plays a vital role in embracing change. By tuning into our thoughts, emotions, and reactions, we can discern whether our resistance to change arises from fear, limiting beliefs, or a genuine need for stability. Self- awareness allows us to respond consciously to change, choosing empowering perspectives and actions that support our growth and well- being.

Change often brings uncertainty and the unknown. Embracing change requires developing trust in ourselves, the process of life, and the universe. Trust serves as an anchor amidst the waves of change, guiding us through periods of transition and helping us embrace the unknown with a sense of curiosity and anticipation. Trust allows us to tap into our inner wisdom and intuition, guiding us towards the paths that align with our highest good.

Embracing change also involves reframing our mindset towards challenges and setbacks. Instead of viewing them as obstacles, we can choose to see them as opportunities for growth and learning. Each challenge presents a chance to develop resilience, expand our capabilities, and uncover hidden strengths. By reframing our perspective, we transform obstacles into stepping stones on our path of self-discovery and personal evolution.

Practicing self-compassion is crucial in the face of change. As we navigate through periods of transformation, we may encounter moments of uncertainty, self-doubt, or discomfort. By offering ourselves kindness, understanding, and acceptance, we create a nurturing space for growth and allow ourselves to embrace the full spectrum of our experiences.

Community and support play a vital role in embracing change. Surrounding ourselves with individuals who uplift and inspire us, seeking guidance from mentors or joining supportive communities can provide encouragement, guidance, and reassurance during times of change. Sharing our experiences and connecting with others on similar journeys fosters a sense of belonging and reminds us that we are not alone in our transformation.

Embracing change also invites us to practice self-reflection and self-reinvention. We have the opportunity to examine our beliefs, values, and aspirations, and consciously choose the paths that align with our authentic selves. Change invites us to shed old identities and patterns that no longer serve us and embrace new versions of ourselves that are more aligned with our true essence.

Ultimately, embracing change is a profound act of self-love and self-empowerment. It allows us to embrace the fullness of life, with all its ups and downs, and surrender to the ever-changing nature of existence. By embracing change, we open ourselves to limitless possibilities, deep transformation, and a life that is continuously evolving and expanding.

So, embrace the fluidity of life. Cultivate openness, trust, and self-awareness. Reframe challenges as opportunities for growth, practice self-compassion, and seek support from your community. Embrace change as a catalyst for personal transformation and reinvention. As you wholeheartedly embrace change, you step into a journey of self-discovery, empowerment, and profound growth, embracing the fluidity of life with grace and resilience.

Transforming challenges into opportunities for growth

Change is an inevitable part of life, and it often brings with it challenges and uncertainties. However, within these challenges lies the potential for profound growth and transformation. In this chapter, we explore the art of embracing change and transforming challenges into opportunities that propel us forward on our journey of personal growth.

When faced with challenges, our first instinct might be to resist or avoid them. But by embracing change and seeing challenges as opportunities, we shift our perspective and open ourselves to transformative possibilities. Embracing change requires a mindset that embraces uncertainty, acknowledges impermanence, and sees challenges as stepping stones on the path of growth.

To transform challenges into opportunities for growth, it is essential to cultivate self-awareness. Take time to reflect on your thoughts, emotions, and reactions when faced with challenges. Observe any patterns of resistance, fear, or self-limiting beliefs that may arise. By becoming aware of these patterns, you can consciously choose to respond with curiosity, openness, and a growth-oriented mindset.

Challenges provide us with valuable lessons and opportunities to develop resilience and inner strength. Instead of viewing challenges as obstacles, reframe them as teachers that invite you to expand your capabilities, learn new skills, and develop a deeper understanding of yourself and the world. Embracing challenges as opportunities for growth empowers you to approach them with a sense of curiosity, courage, and determination.

A key aspect of transforming challenges into opportunities for growth is embracing a growth mindset. Cultivate the belief that your abilities and intelligence can be developed through effort, practice, and learning. Embrace challenges as opportunities to stretch your limits, acquire new knowledge, and refine your skills. By embracing a growth mindset, you view challenges as essential components of your personal and professional development.

Self-compassion is crucial in the process of transforming challenges. Treat yourself with kindness, understanding, and patience when facing difficulties. Acknowledge that challenges are a natural part of life, and it is okay to make mistakes or encounter setbacks. Self-compassion allows you to approach challenges with a sense of gentleness and acceptance, creating a supportive space for growth and transformation.

Seeking support from others can be immensely helpful when navigating challenges. Connect with individuals who provide encouragement, guidance, and wisdom. Share your experiences and challenges with trusted friends, mentors, or support groups. Their perspectives, insights, and experiences can offer fresh perspectives, encouragement, and practical advice, helping you navigate through challenges more effectively.

Embracing change and transforming challenges into opportunities requires a mindset of resilience and adaptability. Remember that change is a natural part of life's ebb and flow. By embracing change, you cultivate the ability to adapt to new circumstances and to see change as an invitation to evolve and expand.

Finally, approach challenges with a sense of gratitude. Each challenge you encounter holds the potential for growth, resilience, and transformation. By viewing challenges as opportunities for personal evolution, you shift your focus to the lessons and blessings they bring. Gratitude opens your heart to the growth that emerges from challenges and allows you to appreciate the journey of transformation.

So, embrace change and transform challenges into opportunities for growth. Cultivate self-awareness, approach challenges with a growth mindset, and practice self-compassion. Seek support from your community, embrace a mindset of resilience, and express gratitude for the lessons learned. As you navigate through challenges with a mindset of growth and transformation, you harness their transformative power and emerge stronger, wiser, and more aligned with your authentic self.

Chapter 10
Beyond Time and Space

Exploring the concepts of timelessness and non-locality

Our perception of reality is often bound by the constraints of time and space. However, there exist realms of existence that transcend these limitations, opening up profound possibilities and insights. In this chapter, we embark on a journey to explore the concepts of timelessness and non-locality, delving into the mysteries that lie beyond our conventional understanding of time and space.

Time, as we commonly perceive it, is a linear progression of moments from past to present to future. But beyond this linear perspective, there is a timeless dimension where past, present, and future coexist in a unified field of consciousness. This timeless realm invites us to explore the interconnectedness of all moments, where the past influences the present, and the present shapes the future. By tapping into this timelessness, we gain access to a profound understanding of the intricate web of existence.

Non-locality refers to the phenomenon in which events and information are not bound by physical distance. In the conventional view of space, objects and information are limited by their proximity. However, in the realm of non-locality, connections and influences can transcend physical boundaries. It suggests that we are interconnected with all things in the universe, and our thoughts, emotions, and actions can have far-reaching effects beyond our immediate surroundings. By embracing non-locality, we recognize our inherent connection to the vastness of existence.

The exploration of timelessness and non-locality requires a shift in our perspective and an expansion of our consciousness. Meditation, mindfulness, and contemplative practices offer pathways to transcend the limitations of time and space. By quieting the mind and entering into a state of deep presence, we can access moments of timelessness and tap into the interconnectedness of all things. These practices invite us to go beyond the constraints of the ordinary mind and open ourselves to expanded states of awareness.

Quantum physics provides insights into the concepts of timelessness and non-locality. Quantum experiments have revealed that particles can be connected in a way that information is instantaneously transmitted between them, regardless of physical distance. These discoveries challenge our traditional understanding of time and space, suggesting that there is a hidden reality beyond what our senses perceive.

In the realm of timelessness and non-locality, the power of consciousness becomes evident. Our thoughts, intentions, and emotions have the ability to shape our reality and influence the interconnected web of existence. By cultivating awareness and directing our consciousness, we become active participants in co-creating our experiences and shaping the world around us.

Exploring timelessness and non-locality invites us to question the nature of our reality and our place within it. It calls us to expand our consciousness and embrace the infinite possibilities that exist beyond the boundaries of time and space. This exploration offers a profound sense of interconnectedness, meaning, and purpose, as we recognize that we are an integral part of a vast cosmic tapestry.

While the concepts of timelessness and non-locality may challenge our conventional understanding, they offer a gateway to a deeper truth and a greater sense of unity. By embracing these concepts, we transcend the limitations of our human perception and awaken to the timeless, interconnected nature of existence.

So, embark on the exploration of timelessness and non-locality. Engage in meditation, mindfulness, and contemplative practices to transcend the constraints of time and space. Embrace the interconnectedness of all things and recognize the power of your consciousness in shaping reality. As you venture beyond the boundaries of time and space, you open yourself to a profound sense of unity, expansiveness, and limitless possibilities that exist within the fabric of existence.

Transcending the limitations of time and space

Our experience of reality is often defined by the boundaries of time and space. However, there are realms of existence that transcend these limitations, inviting us to explore the vast expanses of consciousness and possibilities. In this chapter, we embark on a journey to transcend the constraints of time and space, delving into the mysteries that lie beyond our conventional understanding.

Time, as we perceive it, is a linear progression from past to present to future. But beyond this linear perspective, there exists a timeless dimension where all moments coexist in an eternal now. This timeless realm invites us to transcend the constraints of past and future, and enter into a state of pure presence. By connecting with this timeless dimension, we tap into a profound sense of interconnectedness and gain insights that surpass the limitations of sequential time.

Similarly, our experience of space is often defined by physical boundaries and distances. However, there are dimensions that transcend these spatial limitations. In these expanded realms, distances lose their relevance, and connections occur beyond the constraints of physical proximity. We begin to realize that we are not separate entities confined to individual bodies, but interconnected beings existing in a vast web of consciousness. By transcending the limitations of space, we tap into the inherent unity of all things.

Transcending the limitations of time and space requires a shift in our consciousness. Practices such as meditation, mindfulness, and contemplation provide gateways to this transcendent state. By quieting the mind, letting go of attachment to past and future, and entering into a deep state of presence, we open ourselves to the timeless and boundless nature of our existence. In these states, we can experience glimpses of unity, interconnectedness, and the expansiveness of consciousness beyond the limitations of our physical reality.

Quantum physics offers insights into the nature of reality beyond time and space. Quantum experiments have revealed phenomena such as entanglement and superposition, where particles exist in multiple states simultaneously. These discoveries challenge our traditional understanding of time and space, hinting at the existence of dimensions that transcend our everyday experience. The revelations of quantum physics inspire us to explore the deeper layers of reality and consider the profound possibilities that lie beyond the constraints of our current understanding.

Transcending time and space opens the door to a profound sense of expansion, interconnectedness, and unlimited potential. It invites us to question our perception of reality and our place within it. As we embrace the timeless and boundless nature of existence, we realize that we are not merely limited beings confined to a specific moment or location, but conscious beings with the capacity to explore and create in realms beyond our physical limitations.

By transcending the limitations of time and space, we open ourselves to a greater sense of unity, purpose, and interconnectedness with all beings and aspects of existence. We tap into the infinite well of wisdom and creativity that resides within us, and we align ourselves with the expansive nature of consciousness itself.

So, embark on the journey of transcending time and space. Engage in practices that allow you to enter states of presence and expanded awareness. Explore the revelations of quantum physics and contemplate the mysteries of existence. As you transcend the constraints of time and space, you awaken to the timeless and boundless nature of your being, and you tap into the infinite possibilities and interconnectedness that lie beyond the limitations of our everyday reality.

Chapter 11
Healing and Balancing Energies

Understanding the energy body
and its impact on well- being

Beyond the physical body lies an intricate network of energy that influences our well-being on multiple levels. In this chapter, we explore the concept of the energy body and its profound impact on our physical, emotional, and spiritual health. By understanding and harmonizing our energy, we unlock the potential for healing and holistic well-being.

The energy body, also known as the subtle body or biofield, is composed of various energetic systems that interconnect and interact with our physical body. These systems include the chakras, meridians, aura, and subtle energy centers. Energy flows through these pathways, nourishing and sustaining our overall vitality.

Imbalances or blockages in the energy body can manifest as physical, emotional, or spiritual dis-ease. When the energy flow is disrupted or stagnant, it can lead to symptoms such as fatigue, pain, anxiety, or a feeling of being out of alignment. By recognizing the interconnectedness of our energy body and overall well-being, we can begin to address the root causes of imbalance and restore harmony.

One of the key aspects of healing and balancing energies is understanding the chakra system. Chakras are spinning energy centers located along the central channel of the body. Each chakra corresponds to specific aspects of our being, such as physical health, emotions, communication, intuition, and spiritual connection. By working with the chakras, we can identify and address imbalances, promoting a sense of vitality and well-being.

Practices such as energy healing, meditation, and breathwork offer powerful tools for healing and balancing energies. Energy healing modalities, such as Reiki, Qi Gong, or Pranic Healing, work with the subtle energy systems to restore balance and flow. These practices involve channeling healing energy and removing blockages, facilitating the body's natural ability to heal itself.

Meditation allows us to quiet the mind, cultivate inner stillness, and connect with the subtle realms of our being. By bringing our awareness to the breath, sensations, and energy within the body, we can release tension, clear stagnant energy, and create space for healing and balance to occur. Regular meditation practice promotes overall well-being and supports the harmonization of our energy body.

Breathwork, such as pranayama, helps regulate and balance the flow of life force energy (prana) within our system. Conscious breathing techniques activate the body's natural healing response, promote relaxation, and enhance energy flow. By incorporating breathwork into our daily routine, we can cultivate a deep sense of vitality and presence.

It is essential to pay attention to our energetic boundaries and protect our energy field. We interact with various people, environments, and situations throughout the day, and these interactions can impact our energy. Setting intentions, visualizations, and energetic practices such as aura cleansing or grounding can help create healthy energetic boundaries and shield us from external influences that may disrupt our energy balance.

Another aspect of healing and balancing energies is nurturing our emotional well-being. Emotions carry energy, and unresolved emotions can create imbalances in our energy body. By embracing emotional awareness, processing and expressing our emotions in healthy ways, we release energetic blockages and create space for healing and well-being.

Cultivating self-care practices that support our energetic well-being is essential. Engaging in activities that bring us joy, spending time in nature, nourishing our bodies with wholesome foods, and engaging in creative pursuits all contribute to a harmonious energy body. By nurturing ourselves on all levels, we create an environment that supports healing, balance, and overall well-being.

Understanding and working with our energy body is a holistic approach to health and well-being. By recognizing the interplay between our physical, emotional, and spiritual aspects, we empower ourselves to take an active role in our healing journey. By harmonizing and balancing our energy, we tap into the innate wisdom and vitality that resides within us.

So, embrace the exploration of your energy body. Learn about the chakra system, engage in energy healing modalities, practice meditation and breathwork, and nurture your emotional well-being. Set healthy energetic boundaries and engage in self-care practices that support your energetic well- being. As you understand and balance your energy body, you create a foundation for holistic healing, vitality, and a sense of alignment with your true self.

Techniques for healing and balancing energies

The concept of healing and balancing energies goes beyond mere theory—it is a transformative practice that empowers us to restore harmony and vitality to our being. In this chapter, we explore various techniques that can be utilized for healing and balancing energies, allowing us to enhance our well- being on multiple levels.

1. Energy Healing Modalities: Energy healing modalities such as Reiki, Qi Gong, Pranic Healing, and Healing Touch have been practiced for centuries. These modalities involve channeling healing energy and working with the subtle energy systems of the body to remove blockages, restore balance, and promote overall well-being. Energy healers use their hands, intention, and focused awareness to facilitate the flow of healing energy, supporting the body's natural ability to heal itself.

2. Chakra Balancing: The chakra system is a key aspect of the energy body. Chakras are spinning energy centers located along the central channel of the body, each associated with specific aspects of our being. Balancing the chakras involves identifying and addressing imbalances or blockages in these energy centers. This can be done through visualization, affirmations, sound therapy, crystals, or working with an experienced energy practitioner.

3. Meditation: Meditation is a powerful practice for healing and balancing energies. By quieting the mind, we create a space for deep relaxation and connection with our inner selves. Various meditation techniques can be used, such as mindfulness meditation, guided visualization, or focused breath awareness. Through consistent practice, meditation enhances self-awareness, reduces stress, and promotes a harmonious flow of energy throughout the body.

4. Breathwork: Conscious breathing techniques, known as breathwork, can be used to regulate and balance the flow of life force energy (prana) within the body. Techniques such as deep belly breathing, alternate nostril breathing, or breath of fire activate the body's natural healing response, release tension, and enhance energy flow. Breathwork practices can be incorporated into daily routines or combined with meditation for a more profound healing experience.

5. Sound Healing: Sound has a profound impact on our energy field and can be utilized for healing and balancing energies. Sound healing techniques involve the use of specific frequencies, instruments, or vocal tones to entrain the energy field and promote harmony. Singing bowls, tuning forks, drums, and chanting are commonly used in sound healing practices. By immersing ourselves in these healing sounds, we can release energetic blockages and restore balance.

6. Movement Therapies: Engaging in movement-based therapies such as yoga, Tai Chi, or Qigong can help cultivate a balanced flow of energy. These practices combine physical postures, breathwork, and mindful movement to stimulate energy flow and restore vitality. Through these gentle and flowing movements, we release stagnant energy, enhance flexibility, and cultivate a deep sense of inner peace.

7. Energetic Protection and Clearing: In our daily lives, it is essential to protect our energy field and clear any unwanted or stagnant energies that we may encounter. Techniques such as aura cleansing, grounding, and visualization can help establish healthy energetic boundaries and promote a balanced flow of energy. Regularly clearing and protecting our energy field enables us to maintain a state of equilibrium and prevents the accumulation of negative or draining energies.

8. Emotional Release: Emotions carry energy, and unresolved emotions can create imbalances in our energy body. Engaging in practices that facilitate emotional release, such as journaling, expressive arts, or working with a therapist, allows us to process and express emotions in healthy ways.

By releasing emotional blockages, we create space for healing and balance to occur within our energy field.

Remember that healing and balancing energies is a deeply personal and ongoing journey. It is essential to listen to your intuition and choose the techniques that resonate with you. Explore different practices, seek guidance from experienced practitioners if needed, and establish a regular routine that supports your energetic well-being.

By integrating these techniques into our lives, we empower ourselves to take an active role in our healing journey and cultivate a state of balance, vitality, and alignment with our true selves. Embrace the exploration of healing and balancing energies, and allow these transformative practices to guide you toward greater well-being and a harmonious flow of energy within your being.

Chapter 12
Creating Your Reality

Harnessing the power of intention and manifestation

At the core of our being lies the power to shape our reality. We are co- creators in the intricate tapestry of existence, and our thoughts, beliefs, and intentions have the potential to manifest into tangible experiences. In this chapter, we explore the profound power of intention and manifestation, and how we can consciously create the reality we desire.

1. Clarify Your Intentions: The first step in manifesting your desires is to gain clarity about what you truly want. Take the time to reflect on your deepest desires and aspirations. Write them down, visualize them, and infuse them with positive emotions. The clearer your intentions are, the more focused your energy becomes, aligning you with the frequencies of what you want to manifest.

2. Set Intentions with Purpose: Once you have clarity, set your intentions with purpose and conviction. State them in the present tense, as if they have already manifested. Affirmations and visualizations are powerful tools for programming your subconscious mind and aligning your energy with your intentions. Create a regular practice of repeating your intentions and engaging in visualizations that evoke the feelings and sensations of already having what you desire.

3. Align Your Beliefs and Thoughts: Your beliefs and thoughts play a crucial role in manifesting your reality. Examine any limiting beliefs or doubts that may be holding you back. Challenge and reframe them into empowering

beliefs that support your intentions. Consistently choose thoughts that are aligned with what you want to manifest, and redirect any negative or self-limiting thoughts towards positive and empowering ones. By aligning your beliefs and thoughts with your intentions, you create a fertile ground for manifestation.

4. Take Inspired Action: While intentions and visualization are powerful, they need to be accompanied by inspired action. Act upon the opportunities that come your way and take steps towards your goals. Trust your intuition and follow the guidance that arises from within. Remember, manifestation is a co-creative process, and your inspired actions serve as a bridge between your intentions and their realization.

5. Cultivate Gratitude: Cultivating gratitude is an essential aspect of the manifestation process. Express gratitude for what you already have and for the manifestations that are on their way. Gratitude shifts your focus to abundance, raises your vibrational frequency, and opens the channels for more blessings to flow into your life. Make gratitude a daily practice, and watch as it amplifies your manifestation efforts.

6. Surrender and Trust: While it is important to set intentions and take inspired action, it is equally vital to surrender and trust in the divine timing and unfolding of your manifestations. Release the need for control and attachment to specific outcomes. Trust that the universe is working in your favor and that everything is happening in perfect alignment with your highest good. Surrendering and trusting allow you to enter a state of flow and receptivity, creating space for miracles to occur.

7. Detach from the Outcome: Detaching from the outcome of your manifestations is a paradoxical yet powerful practice. When you detach, you release any resistance or desperation, allowing your intentions to manifest effortlessly. Trust that the universe knows the best way to bring your desires to fruition, even if it may not align with your initial expectations. Detachment allows you to maintain a sense of peace and contentment, regardless of the external circumstances.

8. Reflect and Adjust: Manifestation is an ongoing process that invites continuous reflection and adjustment. Be open to receiving feedback and insights from your experiences. If things are not unfolding as expected, reflect on whether your intentions and actions are in alignment. Adjust your course as needed, and remember that every experience is an opportunity for growth and refinement.

By harnessing the power of intention and manifestation, you become an active participant in co-creating your reality. Trust in the infinite possibilities that exist within and around you. Embrace the process of manifesting with joy, curiosity, and gratitude. As you align your intentions, thoughts, beliefs, and actions, you unlock the inherent power within you to shape a reality that reflects your deepest desires and aspirations.

So, clarify your intentions, set them with purpose, and align your beliefs and thoughts. Take inspired action, cultivate gratitude, and surrender to the flow of manifestation. Detach from the outcome and embrace the journey of co- creation. Reflect, adjust, and remain open to the miracles that unfold. As you harness the power of intention and manifestation, you step into your role as a conscious creator, shaping a reality that aligns with your highest vision and purpose.

Creating a life aligned with your highest vision

Deep within you resides the power to shape your reality and manifest a life that aligns with your highest vision. In this chapter, we explore the transformative process of creating a life that reflects your deepest desires, values, and aspirations. By tapping into your inner wisdom and aligning your actions with your highest vision, you can embark on a journey of conscious creation and experience a fulfilling and purposeful existence.

1. Connect with Your Inner Vision: Begin by connecting with your inner vision, the vision that speaks to the core of who you are and what you truly desire in life. Take time for introspection and self-reflection. What are your passions, values, and dreams? Visualize the life you want to create and allow yourself to feel the emotions associated with that vision. By connecting with your inner vision, you set a powerful intention and establish a guiding compass for your life.

2. Align Your Actions with Your Vision: Creating a life aligned with your highest vision requires consistent action in alignment with your intentions. Break down your vision into smaller, actionable steps and set clear goals that move you closer to your desired reality. Each day, take intentional actions that align with your vision, no matter how small they may seem. Remember that every step counts and contributes to the overall creation of your desired life.

3. Cultivate Self-Belief and Overcome Limiting Beliefs: As you embark on the journey of creating your reality, it is crucial to cultivate self- belief and overcome any limiting beliefs that may hold you back. Identify and challenge the beliefs that undermine your confidence or make you doubt your capabilities. Replace them with empowering beliefs that support your growth and affirm your ability to create the life you desire. Nurture a mindset of possibility, resilience, and unwavering belief in your own potential.

4. Practice Visualization and Affirmations: Visualization and affirmations are powerful tools for manifesting your desired reality. Visualize yourself already living your highest vision in vivid detail, engaging all your senses and emotions. Create a regular practice of affirmations, repeating positive statements that align with your vision and reinforce your belief in its realization. These practices help program your subconscious mind and align your energy with the manifestation of your desires.

5. Embrace Growth and Adaptation: The process of creating your reality is not static; it is a dynamic and ever-evolving journey. Embrace growth and adaptation as integral parts of the process. Be open to learning, exploring new possibilities, and adjusting your path as needed. Stay curious and embrace challenges as opportunities for growth and refinement. Trust that every experience, whether perceived as positive or negative, serves as a catalyst for your evolution and the realization of your highest vision.

6. Surround Yourself with Supportive Connections: Surround yourself with a supportive network of individuals who believe in you, inspire you, and share a similar vision for creating a fulfilling life. Seek out mentors, friends, or communities that can provide guidance, encouragement, and accountability. Share your aspirations with those who will uplift and support you on your journey. Together, you can cultivate an environment that nourishes and sustains your growth and manifestation process.

7. Cultivate Gratitude and Appreciation: Gratitude is a powerful practice that opens the doors for abundance and manifestation. Cultivate a regular gratitude practice, acknowledging and appreciating the blessings and progress along your journey. Gratitude shifts your focus to the present moment and amplifies positive emotions, attracting more reasons to be grateful. By fostering an attitude of gratitude, you create a fertile ground for the manifestation of your highest vision.

8. Trust the Process and Surrender to Divine Timing: Trusting the process and surrendering to divine timing are essential elements of conscious creation. Recognize that there is a

greater intelligence at play, guiding and orchestrating the unfolding of your desires. Trust that everything is happening in perfect alignment with your highest good, even if it may not always align with your expectations. Surrendering allows you to let go of control, release attachment to specific outcomes, and flow with the natural rhythms of life.

By consciously creating a life aligned with your highest vision, you step into your power as a deliberate creator. Embrace the process with dedication, resilience, and self-belief. Align your actions with your vision, overcome limiting beliefs, and cultivate gratitude. Surround yourself with supportive connections, embrace growth and adaptation, and trust the process while surrendering to divine timing. As you embark on this transformative journey, you co-create a life that reflects your true essence, purpose, and highest potential.

Chapter 13
Awakening the Inner Creative Genius

Unlocking your creative potential

Within each of us lies an inner creative genius, a wellspring of inspiration and innovation waiting to be awakened. In this chapter, we delve into the exploration of unlocking your creative potential and tapping into the boundless realms of imagination. By embracing your innate creativity, you can unlock new perspectives, cultivate innovative thinking, and bring forth your unique gifts to the world.

1. Embrace Curiosity and Wonder: Creativity thrives on curiosity and wonder. Cultivate a childlike sense of awe and explore the world with fresh eyes. Allow yourself to ask questions, be open to new experiences, and engage in a lifelong pursuit of learning. Embrace a mindset of continuous curiosity, and let it guide your creative journey.

2. Cultivate a Creative Mindset: Adopt a mindset that embraces possibility and rejects self-imposed limitations. Believe that you have the capacity to be creative in every aspect of your life. Embrace the belief that creativity is not limited to the arts but can be applied to problem-solving, decision-making, and everyday tasks. Let go of perfectionism and embrace experimentation and the freedom to make mistakes. Embrace a growth mindset that recognizes that creativity is a skill that can be developed and nurtured.

3. Create a Supportive Environment: Surround yourself with an environment that nurtures and supports your creative endeavors. Designate a physical space that inspires you and is conducive to your creative process. Surround yourself with objects, artwork, or elements that inspire and

uplift you. Minimize distractions and create a space that encourages focused and uninterrupted creative exploration.

4. Practice Divergent Thinking: Divergent thinking is the ability to generate multiple ideas, perspectives, and solutions. Practice brainstorming sessions, mind mapping, or freewriting to tap into your divergent thinking abilities. Allow your mind to wander and explore unconventional ideas without judgment. Embrace non-linear thinking and seek connections between seemingly unrelated concepts. By practicing divergent thinking, you expand your creative potential and open doors to innovative solutions.

5. Engage in Creative Activities: Actively engage in creative activities that resonate with you. Explore various forms of artistic expression, such as painting, writing, music, dance, or photography. Experiment with different mediums and techniques to discover what sparks your creative fire. Engaging in creative activities not only allows you to express yourself but also helps unlock new perspectives and insights.

6. Embrace Solitude and Reflection: Carve out moments of solitude and reflection in your daily life. These quiet moments provide a fertile ground for creativity to flourish. Disconnect from external distractions and spend time in introspection. Engage in practices such as meditation, journaling, or nature walks to quiet the mind and allow your inner creative voice to emerge.

7. Seek Inspiration from Various Sources: Seek inspiration from diverse sources such as books, art, nature, music, conversations, or travel. Expose yourself to different cultures, perspectives, and disciplines. Explore the works of creative individuals who inspire you and learn from their approaches. By immersing yourself in a rich tapestry of experiences and ideas, you expand your creative palette and gain new insights.

8. Embrace Failure and Perseverance: Failure is an inherent part of the creative process. Embrace failures as learning opportunities and stepping stones to growth. Persevere in the face of setbacks, and view challenges as fuel for your creative journey. Embrace a mindset that celebrates the

process rather than fixating solely on the end result. Embrace the notion that each failure brings you one step closer to uncovering your true creative potential.

9. Collaborate and Share Ideas: Collaboration with others can ignite new ideas and perspectives. Engage in creative collaborations, brainstorming sessions, or group projects. Share your ideas and seek feedback from trusted individuals who support and challenge you. Collaboration not only expands your creative possibilities but also fosters a sense of community and mutual growth.

10. Nurture Self-Care: Self-care is essential for maintaining a balanced and fertile creative mind. Prioritize activities that nourish your physical, mental, and emotional well-being. Engage in practices such as exercise, healthy eating, sufficient rest, and stress management. Cultivate a lifestyle that supports your creative flow and ensures you have the energy and vitality to bring your creative ideas to life.

By embracing your inner creative genius, you awaken a wellspring of inspiration and innovation. Embrace curiosity, cultivate a creative mindset, and create a supportive environment. Practice divergent thinking, engage in creative activities, and embrace solitude for reflection. Seek inspiration from diverse sources, embrace failure and perseverance, and collaborate with others. Nurture self-care and prioritize your well-being. As you unlock your creative potential, you step into a realm of infinite possibilities, expressing your unique gifts and contributing to the beauty and transformation of the world.

Tapping into the limitless wellspring of inspiration

Deep within you lies a wellspring of inspiration, a boundless source of creativity waiting to be awakened. In this chapter, we delve into the exploration of tapping into your inner creative genius, accessing the limitless realm of inspiration that resides within you. By connecting with this wellspring of creativity, you can unleash your unique gifts, foster innovation, and bring forth your creative vision to life.

1. Cultivate Mindfulness and Presence: Creativity flourishes in the present moment. Cultivate mindfulness by bringing your full attention to the here and now. Engage in activities such as meditation, breathwork, or yoga to quiet the mind and heighten your awareness. By grounding yourself in the present moment, you create space for inspiration to flow effortlessly.

2. Cultivate a Curious Mind: Embrace a mindset of curiosity and open- mindedness. Approach life with a childlike sense of wonder, always seeking new experiences and perspectives. Ask questions, explore diverse topics, and delve into areas outside your comfort zone. By nurturing a curious mind, you open yourself up to a wealth of inspiration and possibilities.

3. Embrace Solitude and Silence: Find moments of solitude and silence to tap into your inner wellspring of inspiration. Create a tranquil space where you can retreat from the external noise and distractions of everyday life. Allow yourself to simply be, without the need for constant stimulation. In this stillness, you can access the depths of your creative potential.

4. Engage in Creative Rituals: Develop creative rituals that signal to your mind and spirit that it's time to tap into your creative genius. Establish a consistent creative practice,

whether it's writing, painting, dancing, or any other form of artistic expression. Create a dedicated space and time for your creative pursuits, making it a priority in your life.

5. Surround Yourself with Inspiration: Surround yourself with sources of inspiration that resonate with your creative vision. Immerse yourself in art, music, literature, nature, or any other medium that ignites your imagination. Seek out individuals who inspire and challenge you, creating a supportive network of fellow creatives. The energy and ideas of others can fuel your own creative fire.

6. Engage in Active Observation: Cultivate the art of observation in your daily life. Pay attention to the details, textures, colors, sounds, and emotions present in your surroundings. Be fully present and engage your senses. By actively observing the world around you, you develop a heightened awareness that can spark fresh ideas and novel insights.

7. Embrace Risk and Experimentation: Creativity thrives when you embrace risk and step outside of your comfort zone. Be willing to take chances, explore new ideas, and experiment with different approaches. Embrace failures as opportunities for growth and learning. By pushing the boundaries of what is familiar, you open yourself up to new possibilities and creative breakthroughs.

8. Embody Authenticity: Your inner creative genius flourishes when you embrace your authentic self. Embody your unique voice, values, and vision. Celebrate your strengths and embrace your imperfections. Trust in your intuition and allow it to guide your creative expression. By being true to yourself, you tap into a wellspring of inspiration that is uniquely yours.

9. Embrace Collaboration and Feedback: Collaboration with others can amplify your creative potential. Seek out opportunities to collaborate with like-minded individuals who share your passion for creativity.

Engage in constructive feedback exchanges, valuing different perspectives and insights. Embracing collaboration and feedback enriches your creative process and fuels further inspiration.

10. Engage in Continuous Learning: Commit to a lifelong journey of learning and growth. Explore new fields of knowledge, acquire new skills, and challenge yourself intellectually. Attend workshops, take courses, or engage in self-study to expand your understanding of the world. The pursuit of knowledge opens doors to new insights and perspectives, fueling your creative genius.

By tapping into the limitless wellspring of inspiration within you, you awaken your inner creative genius. Cultivate mindfulness, embrace curiosity, and find solace in solitude. Engage in creative rituals, surround yourself with inspiration, and actively observe the world. Embrace risk, authenticity, collaboration, and continuous learning. As you tap into this infinite source of inspiration, you unlock your creative genius, bringing forth your unique gifts and making a profound impact on the world around you.

Chapter 14
The Dance of Synchronicity

Recognizing and embracing synchronicities in life

Life is a tapestry of interconnected events and meaningful coincidences that weave together in a beautiful dance of synchronicity. In this chapter, we explore the fascinating phenomenon of synchronicity and its profound impact on our lives. By recognizing and embracing synchronicities, we can tap into the flow of universal wisdom and guidance, opening ourselves to new possibilities and deeper connections.

1. Understanding Synchronicity: Synchronicity is the occurrence of seemingly unrelated events that hold significant meaning when they align in a meaningful way. These synchronicities often defy rational explanation, appearing as meaningful coincidences or serendipitous encounters. They can take the form of symbols, numbers, unexpected meetings, or a series of events that align with our thoughts or intentions. By recognizing synchronicities, we glimpse the underlying interconnectedness of the universe.

2. Cultivating Awareness: Developing awareness is key to recognizing synchronicities in our lives. Slow down and pay attention to the present moment. Be fully present in your interactions and environment, allowing your senses to be receptive to the subtle signs and messages around you. Cultivate a sense of curiosity and wonder, as synchronicities often reveal themselves when we approach life with an open and receptive mindset.

3. Trusting Your Intuition: Intuition is a powerful tool for recognizing and interpreting synchronicities. Tune into

your inner guidance and trust the intuitive nudges that arise within you. Your intuition acts as a compass, directing you toward meaningful synchronistic experiences. Practice listening to your inner voice and follow the guidance it provides. As you trust your intuition, you open yourself to the flow of synchronicity in your life.

4. Reflecting on Personal Meaning: Synchronicities carry personal meaning that resonates deeply with us. Take time to reflect on the messages and symbolism that synchronistic events bring forth. Consider the emotions, thoughts, or circumstances surrounding the synchronicity. Journaling, meditation, or contemplative practices can help you explore the personal significance of these meaningful coincidences. Reflecting on their meaning allows you to integrate the wisdom and guidance they offer.

5. Embracing the Unfolding Path: Synchronicities often occur as signposts guiding us along our life's journey. Embrace the unfolding path and trust that synchronicities are there to guide you toward your highest good. They may come as affirmations, gentle nudges, or even redirections. Surrender to the flow of synchronicity, and allow it to guide you toward new opportunities, connections, and experiences.

6. Co-creating with the Universe: Synchronicity is a dance between our intentions, actions, and the universe's response. Set clear intentions and engage in inspired actions aligned with your desires and purpose. As you actively participate in the co-creation process, you amplify the occurrence of synchronicities in your life. Embrace a mindset of co-creation, knowing that you are an active participant in the dance of synchronicity.

7. Gratitude and Appreciation: Cultivate an attitude of gratitude for the synchronicities that grace your life. Express appreciation for the connections, guidance, and meaningful encounters that unfold. Gratitude amplifies the flow of synchronicity, attracting more instances of meaningful coincidences. As you express gratitude for the synchronicities, you deepen your connection to the abundant tapestry of the universe.

8. Sharing and Connecting: Synchronicities often occur in the context of connections with others. Share your synchronistic experiences with trusted friends, family, or like-minded communities. Engage in conversations that explore the magic and mystery of synchronicity. Connecting with others who have experienced synchronicities can deepen your understanding and provide validation, creating a sense of belonging within this interconnected web of meaningful coincidences.

9. Integrating Synchronicities into Daily Life: Embrace synchronicities as an integral part of your daily life. Develop a practice of actively seeking out and acknowledging synchronicities. Keep a synchronicity journal to record and reflect upon these meaningful events. Incorporate rituals or practices that honor and invite synchronicity into your life, such as meditation, affirmations, or setting intentions. By integrating synchronicities into your daily life, you create a space for greater awareness and alignment with the universal flow.

10. Trusting the Process: Above all, trust in the process of synchronicity.

Trust that the universe is intricately woven together, guiding and supporting you on your journey. Even when synchronicities may seem unclear or puzzling in the moment, trust that they are part of a larger unfolding tapestry of your life. Trust that everything is happening in perfect timing and alignment with your soul's growth and evolution.

By recognizing and embracing synchronicities, you tap into the interconnected nature of the universe. Cultivate awareness, trust your intuition, and reflect on personal meaning. Embrace the unfolding path, co- create with the universe, and express gratitude for the synchronicities in your life. Share and connect with others, integrate synchronicities into your daily life, and trust in the process. As you embrace the dance of synchronicity, you align with the universal flow and invite a deeper sense of purpose, connection, and meaning into your life.

Harnessing their guidance and significance

In the intricate dance of life, synchronicity emerges as a beautiful and mysterious partner, guiding us along our journey with meaningful coincidences and profound connections. In this chapter, we explore the power of synchronicity and how we can harness its guidance and significance in our lives. By recognizing and embracing synchronicities, we open ourselves to a deeper level of awareness, insight, and alignment with the greater flow of existence.

1. The Language of Synchronicity: Synchronicity speaks to us in a language beyond words. It is the symphony of events, encounters, and signs that seemingly align without logical explanation. Pay attention to the signs and symbols that cross your path—an unexpected meeting, a recurring number, a meaningful coincidence. These are the whispers of synchronicity, inviting us to delve deeper into their significance.

2. Cultivating Awareness: Awareness is the key to recognizing and harnessing the power of synchronicity. Cultivate a mindful presence in your daily life. Be fully engaged in the present moment, receptive to the subtle messages and connections that unfold around you. Slow down, observe, and listen—to your surroundings, to your intuition, and to the synchronicities that emerge. The more you cultivate awareness, the more synchronicities you will perceive.

3. Trusting Your Inner Guidance: Your intuition is a potent ally in navigating the dance of synchronicity. Trust the wisdom that arises from within. When a synchronistic event occurs, tune into your intuition and sense the significance it holds for you. Allow your inner guidance to lead you towards deeper understanding and insight. Trusting your intuition helps you align with the flow of synchronicity and navigate your path with greater clarity.

4. Following the Threads: Synchronicities often appear as interconnected threads woven into the fabric of our lives. Pay attention to the patterns and connections that emerge between synchronistic events. Notice how one event leads to another, seemingly guiding you towards a specific direction or revelation. By following these threads, you uncover hidden insights, opportunities, and transformative experiences.

5. Reflecting on Meaning: Each synchronicity carries a unique message and meaning for us. Take the time to reflect on the significance of these events in your life. Journaling, meditation, or contemplation can help you explore the personal and symbolic meanings behind synchronicities. Consider the emotions, thoughts, and circumstances surrounding the synchronistic event. Through reflection, you gain deeper insight into their relevance and the guidance they offer.

6. Co-creating with Synchronicity: Synchronicity is not merely a random occurrence; it is a co-creative dance between you and the universe. Set clear intentions and engage in inspired action aligned with your desires. Take steps towards your goals, remaining open to the guidance and opportunities that synchronicity presents. By actively participating in this dance, you align yourself with the universal flow and invite synchronicity to shape your journey.

7. Gratitude and Appreciation: Express gratitude for the synchronicities that grace your life. Appreciate the guidance, connections, and insights they bring. Gratitude deepens your connection to the flow of synchronicity, amplifying its presence in your life. Embrace an attitude of appreciation for the intricate dance of events that align for your growth and well-being.

8. Trusting the Process: Trust in the unfolding of synchronicity. Even if you don't immediately understand the meaning or purpose behind a synchronistic event, trust that it serves a greater purpose in your life. Trust that everything is happening in divine timing and alignment with your highest good. Surrender the need to control or

analyze every aspect, and allow the dance of synchronicity to guide you with its wisdom.

9. Integration and Application: Synchronicity is not meant to be merely observed; it is meant to be integrated into your life. Take the lessons and insights gained from synchronistic events and apply them to your daily experiences. Allow synchronicity to guide your decisions, relationships, and actions. By actively integrating the wisdom of synchronicity, you create a life in alignment with its flow and guidance.

10. Embracing the Journey: Synchronicity is an invitation to embrace the journey of life with awe and wonder. Embrace the mystery and magic that unfolds in each synchronistic encounter. View every synchronicity as an opportunity for growth, expansion, and deeper connection with the greater web of existence. Embrace the dance of synchronicity with an open heart, and allow it to infuse your life with joy, meaning, and purpose.

By recognizing and harnessing synchronicity, you tap into a profound source of guidance and significance. Cultivate awareness, trust your intuition, and follow the threads of synchronicity. Reflect on their meaning, co-create with the universe, and express gratitude for their presence. Trust the process, integrate their lessons, and embrace the journey with awe and wonder. As you dance with synchronicity, you align yourself with the deeper currents of life, experiencing a profound sense of interconnectedness, purpose, and fulfillment.

Chapter 15
Embodying Unconditional Love

Cultivating love and compassion for self and others

Love is the essence that connects all beings, transcending boundaries and uniting us in a profound and transformative way. In this chapter, we explore the power of unconditional love and how we can embody it in our lives. By cultivating love and compassion for ourselves and extending it to others, we create a ripple effect of healing, kindness, and connection.

1. Understanding Unconditional Love: Unconditional love is a boundless and accepting love that transcends conditions and expectations. It is a love that embraces the totality of who we are, with all our strengths, weaknesses, and imperfections. Recognize that you are inherently worthy of love and deserving of self-compassion, regardless of external achievements or circumstances. Embrace the understanding that all beings are deserving of love and compassion, regardless of their flaws or mistakes.

2. Cultivating Self-Love: Begin by cultivating a deep sense of love and compassion for yourself. Nurture self-care practices that honor your physical, emotional, and spiritual well-being. Practice self-acceptance and self-forgiveness, releasing judgment and embracing your authentic self. Engage in activities that bring you joy and fulfillment. Treat yourself with kindness, gentleness, and respect, as you would treat a dear friend. By cultivating self-love, you create a solid foundation for extending love to others.

3. Practicing Self-Compassion: Self-compassion is a vital aspect of embodying unconditional love. When faced

with challenges or setbacks, offer yourself kindness, understanding, and support. Embrace self-compassionate language and thoughts, replacing self-criticism with self-encouragement. Acknowledge that making mistakes and facing difficulties are part of the human experience. Treat yourself with patience and empathy, knowing that you are doing the best you can in each moment.

4. Cultivating Empathy and Compassion: Extend your love and compassion to others by cultivating empathy and compassion. Practice placing yourself in another person's shoes, seeking to understand their experiences and perspectives. Listen deeply and attentively when others share their joys, sorrows, or struggles. Respond with kindness, empathy, and non-judgment. Cultivate a compassionate heart that recognizes the interconnectedness of all beings.

5. Practicing Loving-Kindness Meditation: Engage in loving-kindness meditation as a practice to cultivate love and compassion for yourself and others. Set aside dedicated time each day to sit in stillness and send loving-kindness to yourself, loved ones, acquaintances, and even challenging individuals. Visualize each person receiving love, happiness, and well-being. As you extend love through this practice, you open your heart to the transformative power of unconditional love.

6. Forgiveness and Letting Go: Embrace the practice of forgiveness as a pathway to unconditional love. Release any resentment, grudges, or judgments you may hold towards yourself or others. Understand that forgiveness is not condoning harmful actions but rather freeing yourself from the burden of carrying negative emotions. By forgiving and letting go, you create space for love and compassion to flow freely.

7. Engaging in Acts of Kindness: Embody unconditional love through acts of kindness and service. Seek opportunities to help, support, or uplift others in need. Engage in random acts of kindness, no matter how small. Offer a listening ear, a helping hand, or a simple act of generosity. By practicing

kindness, you foster a sense of connection, empathy, and compassion.

8. Embracing Vulnerability: Unconditional love requires embracing vulnerability, both within ourselves and in our relationships. Be willing to open your heart, express your authentic emotions, and allow yourself to be seen for who you truly are. Cultivate deep connections with others based on trust, honesty, and vulnerability. Embracing vulnerability creates a space for genuine love and compassion to flourish.

9. Practicing Non-Judgment: Release the habit of judgment towards yourself and others. Recognize that everyone is on their unique journey, facing their own challenges and growth opportunities. Practice seeing the inherent goodness in all beings, even when their actions may seem misguided. Embrace a non-judgmental attitude that allows love and compassion to flow freely.

10. Gratitude and Appreciation: Cultivate an attitude of gratitude and appreciation for the abundance of love and compassion in your life. Express gratitude for the love you receive from others, as well as the opportunities to extend love to others. Foster a daily practice of acknowledging and appreciating the presence of love in all its forms. Gratitude deepens your connection to the essence of unconditional love.

By embodying unconditional love, you tap into the transformative power of love and compassion. Cultivate self-love, practice self-compassion, and extend empathy and compassion to others. Engage in loving-kindness meditation, forgive and let go, and engage in acts of kindness. Embrace vulnerability, practice non-judgment, and cultivate gratitude and appreciation. As you embody unconditional love, you become a beacon of light, creating a ripple effect of healing, kindness, and connection in the world.

Embodying the essence of unconditional love

Unconditional love is the purest and most transformative force that exists. It transcends limitations, embraces all beings, and radiates from the depths of our being. In this chapter, we explore the profound journey of embodying unconditional love and becoming a vessel for its boundless expression. By cultivating this divine essence within ourselves, we awaken to the limitless power of love and its ability to heal, transform, and uplift the world.

1. Recognizing the Essence of Unconditional Love: Unconditional love is the unbounded, all-encompassing essence that resides within each of us. It is a love that transcends judgment, conditions, and expectations. Recognize that this love is your true nature, an eternal flame that burns brightly within your heart. Understand that embodying unconditional love is a journey of self-discovery and remembrance.

2. Releasing Fear and Opening the Heart: Embodying unconditional love requires releasing the shackles of fear that inhibit its expression. Open your heart to vulnerability and let go of the walls and defenses that prevent love from flowing freely. Face your fears with compassion and courage, knowing that love is the antidote that dissolves all barriers. As you release fear, your heart expands, and the essence of unconditional love blossoms within you.

3. Cultivating Self-Love and Self-Acceptance: Embodying unconditional love starts with cultivating deep love and acceptance for yourself. Recognize your inherent worthiness and embrace the totality of who you are, including your strengths, weaknesses, and imperfections. Practice self-care, self-compassion, and self-forgiveness. Treat yourself with kindness, gentleness, and respect. By nourishing self-love, you create a solid foundation for extending love to others.

4. Extending Love and Compassion: Embodying unconditional love involves extending it beyond yourself to all beings. Cultivate compassion for others by acknowledging their inherent worthiness and recognizing their unique journeys. Practice empathy, actively listening, and seeking to understand the experiences of others. Extend acts of kindness, support, and generosity to those in need. By extending love and compassion, you become a conduit for its transformative power.

5. Practicing Forgiveness and Letting Go: Forgiveness is a cornerstone of unconditional love. Release resentment, grudges, and judgments held towards yourself and others. Understand that forgiveness is a liberating act of self-healing and an expression of love's boundless nature. By forgiving and letting go, you create space for love to flow freely, allowing healing and transformation to unfold.

6. Embracing Unity and Interconnectedness: Embodying unconditional love involves embracing the truth of unity and interconnectedness. Recognize that all beings are interconnected, part of the vast tapestry of life. Embrace the understanding that hurting another is hurting oneself, and that the well-being of one is intimately connected to the well-being of all. Cultivate a sense of oneness and compassion for the collective human family, as well as for all living beings and the Earth itself.

7. Practicing Mindful Presence and Conscious Actions: Embodying unconditional love is rooted in mindful presence and conscious actions. Cultivate awareness of your thoughts, words, and deeds. Practice mindfulness in every interaction, infusing them with love, kindness, and compassion. Choose actions that reflect the essence of unconditional love, promoting harmony, understanding, and well-being. As you live with conscious intention, you become an embodiment of love in action.

8. Surrendering to the Flow of Love: Surrender to the flow of love and trust in its divine intelligence. Let go of the need to control or manipulate, and instead allow love to guide your thoughts, emotions, and actions. Surrendering opens you to the limitless possibilities and miracles that unfold when you

align with the current of love. By surrendering, you become an instrument of love's expression in the world.

9. Embracing Gratitude and Appreciation: Cultivate an attitude of gratitude and appreciation for the beauty and abundance of love in your life. Express gratitude for the love you receive from others, as well as for the opportunities to give and receive love. Practice appreciating the simple joys, acts of kindness, and moments of connection that are infused with the essence of unconditional love. Gratitude deepens your connection to the wellspring of love within you.

10. Radiating Love into the World: Embodying unconditional love means becoming a radiant presence of love in the world. Let your love shine through your words, actions, and presence. Infuse love into your relationships, your work, and your interactions with all beings. Share your love freely, without attachment or expectation. As you radiate love, you inspire others to awaken to their own capacity for unconditional love.

By embodying the essence of unconditional love, you become a living embodiment of its transformative power. Release fear and open your heart. Cultivate self-love and extend love and compassion to others. Practice forgiveness and embrace unity. Live with mindful presence and conscious actions. Surrender to the flow of love and embrace gratitude. Radiate love into the world, igniting a ripple effect of healing and transformation. As you embody unconditional love, you become a beacon of light, inspiring others to embrace the boundless power of love within themselves.

Chapter 16
Expanding Conscious Relationships

Nurturing conscious and meaningful connections

Human connections are the threads that weave the tapestry of our lives, shaping our experiences and influencing our growth. In this chapter, we explore the beauty and transformative power of expanding conscious relationships. By cultivating awareness, authenticity, and compassion, we can nurture deep and meaningful connections that honor the essence of each individual and foster mutual growth and fulfillment.

1. Embracing Conscious Awareness: Cultivate conscious awareness in your relationships by being fully present and engaged. Practice active listening, giving your undivided attention to others. Be mindful of your thoughts, words, and actions, choosing to respond rather than react. By embodying conscious awareness, you create a foundation for authentic and meaningful connections.

2. Honoring Authenticity: Embrace your authenticity and invite others to do the same. Be true to yourself and allow others to express themselves freely without judgment or expectations. Encourage open and honest communication, creating a safe space for vulnerability and sharing. Embracing authenticity in relationships fosters trust and deepens connections.

3. Practicing Empathy and Compassion: Cultivate empathy and compassion in your relationships. Seek to understand others' perspectives, experiences, and emotions. Practice placing yourself in their shoes, suspending judgment, and offering understanding and support. Compassion is a

bridge that connects hearts, fostering deeper connections and healing.

4. Embracing Vulnerability: Embrace vulnerability as a pathway to authentic connections. Share your joys, fears, dreams, and struggles with those you trust. Allow yourself to be seen in your raw, imperfect state, knowing that true connections are formed when we are willing to show up as our genuine selves. Embracing vulnerability invites others to do the same, deepening the bond of trust and understanding.

5. Cultivating Communication Skills: Enhance your communication skills to foster conscious relationships. Practice active listening, seeking clarification when needed, and expressing yourself with clarity and compassion. Strive for nonviolent communication, using "I" statements and focusing on observations, feelings, needs, and requests. Effective communication builds bridges of understanding and cultivates harmonious connections.

6. Embodying Equality and Mutual Respect: Foster relationships based on equality and mutual respect. Recognize and honor the inherent worth and dignity of each individual. Embrace diversity, valuing different perspectives and experiences. Avoid power dynamics and strive for collaboration, cooperation, and shared decision-making. Embodying equality and mutual respect creates a nurturing environment for conscious connections to flourish.

7. Cultivating Gratitude and Appreciation: Cultivate gratitude and appreciation for the presence and contributions of others in your life. Express your gratitude openly and sincerely. Celebrate their strengths, achievements, and unique qualities. By cultivating gratitude and appreciation, you foster an atmosphere of positivity and connection.

8. Embracing Conflict Resolution and Growth: Conflict is a natural part of any relationship. Embrace conflict as an opportunity for growth and understanding. Practice compassionate and constructive conflict resolution. Engage in active listening, seek to understand the underlying needs and emotions, and work towards mutually beneficial solutions. Embracing conflict as a catalyst for growth strengthens the foundation of conscious relationships.

9. Cultivating Shared Values and Purpose: Nurture relationships with individuals who share your values and purpose. Seek connections with like-minded individuals who inspire and challenge you to grow. Engage in activities and projects that align with your shared values and contribute to a greater purpose. Cultivating shared values and purpose deepens the connection and creates a sense of belonging and fulfillment.

10. Engaging in Rituals and Practices: Create rituals and practices that deepen the connection in your relationships. Engage in shared activities that nourish the bond, such as shared meals, walks in nature, or creative collaborations. Explore practices like meditation, mindfulness, or gratitude exercises together. Rituals and practices provide a sacred space to connect, reflect, and grow.

By expanding conscious relationships, you create a rich tapestry of meaningful connections in your life. Embrace conscious awareness, honor authenticity, and practice empathy and compassion. Embrace vulnerability, cultivate effective communication, and embody equality and mutual respect. Cultivate gratitude and appreciation, embrace conflict resolution, and nurture shared values and purpose. Engage in rituals and practices that deepen connections. As you nurture conscious relationships, you cultivate a supportive network that uplifts and inspires you, fostering growth, love, and fulfillment in your life and the lives of others.

Transforming relationships through awareness and authenticity

Our relationships hold the potential for deep connection, growth, and transformation. In this chapter, we explore how we can expand our conscious relationships by cultivating awareness and authenticity. By bringing a mindful presence and genuine self-expression into our connections, we can create spaces of love, understanding, and profound evolution.

1. Cultivating Self-Awareness: Begin by cultivating self-awareness, as it forms the foundation for expanding conscious relationships. Take time to reflect on your thoughts, emotions, and patterns of behavior. Explore your values, beliefs, and desires. By understanding yourself at a deeper level, you gain clarity and can approach relationships with authenticity and integrity.

2. Mindful Presence: Practice bringing a mindful presence into your relationships. Be fully present and engaged, giving your complete attention to the person in front of you. Let go of distractions and judgments. Listen with an open heart, seeking to understand rather than to respond. By being present, you create space for deeper connection and authentic communication.

3. Authentic Self-Expression: Embrace authenticity in your relationships by expressing yourself honestly and vulnerably. Share your thoughts, feelings, and desires openly, without fear of judgment or rejection. Allow your true self to be seen and heard. Authentic self-expression creates an environment where trust can flourish and deeper connections can be formed.

4. Active Listening: Practice active listening as a way to honor and understand others. Give your full attention to the person speaking, without interrupting or planning your response. Seek to understand their perspective, emotions,

and needs. Validate their experiences and create a safe space for them to express themselves. Active listening nurtures empathy, deepens understanding, and fosters meaningful connections.

5. Compassion and Empathy: Cultivate compassion and empathy in your relationships. Recognize that each person carries their own joys, sorrows, and struggles. Seek to understand their experiences and emotions. Extend kindness and support, even in difficult moments. By practicing compassion and empathy, you create a nurturing environment for growth and healing.

6. Embracing Vulnerability: Embrace vulnerability as a catalyst for deepening connections. Allow yourself to be seen and known, including your fears, insecurities, and imperfections. Create a safe space for others to express their vulnerability as well. In vulnerability, walls are broken down, and authentic bonds are forged. Embracing vulnerability strengthens relationships and cultivates trust.

7. Honoring Boundaries: Respect and honor the boundaries of yourself and others. Communicate your boundaries clearly and assertively, and respect the boundaries set by others. Boundaries create a sense of safety and respect within relationships. By honoring boundaries, you foster healthy dynamics and mutual understanding.

8. Cultivating Acceptance: Practice acceptance in your relationships, embracing others for who they are without trying to change them. Recognize that everyone is on their unique journey of growth and self- discovery. Release the need for control or expectations, allowing space for acceptance and understanding to thrive. Cultivating acceptance creates an environment of non-judgment and love.

9. Communication and Conflict Resolution: Foster open and honest communication within your relationships. Express yourself with clarity, compassion, and respect. When conflicts arise, engage in constructive conflict resolution. Listen attentively, seek to understand the underlying needs and emotions, and work towards mutually beneficial

solutions. Effective communication and conflict resolution deepen understanding and strengthen relationships.

10. Cultivating Growth and Evolution: View relationships as opportunities for growth and evolution. Support each other's personal development and encourage exploration of new perspectives and experiences. Celebrate successes and navigate challenges together. Embrace change and transformation as natural aspects of relationships. Cultivating growth and evolution nourishes the dynamic nature of conscious connections.

By expanding conscious relationships, we invite profound transformation into our lives. Cultivate self-awareness, practice mindful presence, and embrace authentic self-expression. Engage in active listening, compassion, and empathy. Embrace vulnerability and honor boundaries. Cultivate acceptance and practice open communication and conflict resolution. Cultivate growth and evolution within relationships. As you bring awareness and authenticity into your connections, you create spaces of love, understanding, and profound transformation, enriching the lives of all involved.

Chapter 17
The Unity of Body, Mind, and Spirit

Recognizing the interplay between the physical, mental, and spiritual aspects of self

In our journey of self-discovery and growth, it is essential to recognize the profound interplay between the body, mind, and spirit. In this chapter, we explore the unity of these aspects of self and how their harmonious integration can lead to a deeper sense of well-being, purpose, and fulfillment. By acknowledging and nurturing the interconnectedness of our physical, mental, and spiritual dimensions, we can experience greater wholeness and alignment in our lives.

1. Understanding the Three Dimensions: The body, mind, and spirit are inseparable aspects of our being. The body represents our physical form, sensations, and vitality. The mind encompasses our thoughts, emotions, beliefs, and perceptions. The spirit embodies our essence, consciousness, and connection to something greater than ourselves. Recognize that each dimension influences and interacts with the others, forming a holistic framework for our experience of life.

2. Honoring the Physical Body: Begin by honoring and caring for your physical body. Nurture it through nourishing food, regular movement, restful sleep, and mindful self-care practices. Cultivate a sense of body awareness and listen to its signals and needs. Recognize that the body is a sacred vessel that houses your essence and serves as a vehicle for your experiences in this physical realm.

3. Cultivating Mental Well-being: Pay attention to your mental well-being and cultivate a positive and empowering

mindset. Practice mindfulness to observe and understand your thoughts. Challenge negative or limiting beliefs and replace them with empowering ones. Engage in activities that stimulate your intellect and creativity. Cultivate gratitude and optimism to nourish a positive mental outlook.

4. Nurturing Emotional Balance: Embrace and honor your emotions as valuable messengers and guides. Allow yourself to feel and express a wide range of emotions without judgment or suppression. Practice emotional self-regulation by cultivating awareness and healthy coping mechanisms. Seek support when needed, whether through therapy, counseling, or trusted relationships. Nurturing emotional balance allows for greater harmony and well-being in all aspects of life.

5. Connecting with the Spirit: Cultivate a deeper connection with your spiritual essence. Explore practices that resonate with your beliefs, such as meditation, prayer, contemplation, or nature immersion. Engage in activities that nourish your soul and bring you closer to a sense of meaning and purpose. Recognize that spirituality is a personal journey, and embrace practices that align with your unique path.

6. Integration and Alignment: Recognize that true well-being and fulfillment arise from the integration and alignment of the body, mind, and spirit. Seek practices and experiences that facilitate this integration, such as yoga, tai chi, dance, or energy work. Engage in activities that bring joy, creativity, and inspiration, fostering a sense of alignment and unity within yourself.

7. Listening to Inner Wisdom: Cultivate the practice of tuning into your inner wisdom. Create moments of stillness and silence to listen to the whispers of your intuition and higher self. Trust the guidance that arises from within and allow it to inform your choices, actions, and relationships. The more you listen to your inner wisdom, the more aligned and harmonious your life becomes.

8. Living with Intention: Set clear intentions that honor the unity of your body, mind, and spirit. Align your actions with these intentions, making conscious choices that support your overall well-being and growth. Let your intentions

guide your daily practices, relationships, and life's purpose. Living with intention brings clarity, focus, and a sense of purpose to your journey.

9. Seeking Balance: Strive for balance among the body, mind, and spirit.

Avoid extremes and honor the unique needs of each dimension. Find a rhythm that allows for self-care, self-reflection, and spiritual nourishment alongside the demands of daily life. Cultivate practices and routines that support balance and harmony among these dimensions.

10. Embracing the Journey: Embrace the ongoing journey of integrating and aligning the body, mind, and spirit. Recognize that this is a lifelong process of self-discovery, growth, and transformation. Be patient and compassionate with yourself along the way, knowing that each step forward brings you closer to a deeper sense of wholeness and unity.

By recognizing the interplay between the body, mind, and spirit, we can cultivate a greater sense of well-being, purpose, and fulfillment. Honor and care for your physical body, cultivate mental well-being, nurture emotional balance, and connect with your spiritual essence. Seek integration and alignment among these dimensions, listening to your inner wisdom and living with intention. Strive for balance and embrace the ongoing journey of unity among the body, mind, and spirit. As you foster this integration, you experience a profound sense of wholeness, alignment, and connectedness to the essence of your being.

Cultivating harmony and integration within

The unity of the body, mind, and spirit is a profound and transformative journey of self-discovery and growth. In this chapter, we explore the importance of cultivating harmony and integration within these dimensions of our being. By nurturing a deep sense of unity, we can experience greater well-being, balance, and fulfillment in our lives.

1. Recognizing the Interconnectedness: Begin by recognizing the inherent interconnectedness of your body, mind, and spirit. Understand that they are not separate entities but are deeply intertwined aspects of your whole being. Each dimension influences and impacts the others, creating a holistic framework for your experience of life. Embrace the understanding that when one aspect thrives, the others are also positively affected.

2. Honoring the Body: Cultivate a deep respect and appreciation for your physical body. Recognize it as a sacred vessel that houses your essence and allows you to navigate the physical world. Nourish your body with nutritious food, regular exercise, and adequate rest. Listen to its signals and respond with care and compassion. Treat your body as a temple, honoring its unique needs and supporting its vitality.

3. Cultivating Mental Clarity: Cultivate mental clarity and well-being by nurturing a positive and empowered mindset. Practice mindfulness to observe your thoughts without judgment. Challenge limiting beliefs and replace them with empowering ones. Engage in activities that stimulate your intellect and creativity. Cultivate gratitude and optimism to foster a positive mental outlook. As you cultivate mental clarity, you create a foundation for harmony and integration.

4. Nurturing Emotional Intelligence: Embrace and honor your emotions as valuable messengers and guides. Develop emotional intelligence by becoming aware of your emotions

and their underlying causes. Learn to express and manage your emotions in healthy and constructive ways. Cultivate empathy and compassion towards yourself and others. By nurturing emotional intelligence, you create space for emotional harmony and integration.

5. Connecting with the Spirit: Cultivate a deeper connection with your spiritual essence. Engage in practices that resonate with your beliefs and values, such as meditation, prayer, contemplation, or spending time in nature. Nurture a sense of awe and wonder for the mysteries of life. Seek experiences that bring you closer to your spiritual essence and provide a sense of meaning and purpose. Connecting with the spirit nourishes your innermost being and fosters a sense of unity.

6. Integration and Alignment: Strive for integration and alignment among your body, mind, and spirit. Recognize that they are not separate entities but are meant to work in harmony. Engage in activities that facilitate their integration, such as yoga, tai chi, breathwork, or dance. Create rituals or practices that allow you to bring them into alignment, such as meditation or journaling. By consciously integrating and aligning these dimensions, you create a state of wholeness and unity within yourself.

7. Listening to Inner Wisdom: Cultivate the practice of listening to your inner wisdom. Create moments of stillness and silence to tune in and connect with your intuitive guidance. Trust the wisdom that arises from within and allow it to guide your decisions, actions, and relationships. By listening to your inner wisdom, you align yourself with the inherent harmony and integration of your being.

8. Seeking Balance: Strive for balance among your body, mind, and spirit.

Avoid extremes and honor the unique needs of each dimension. Cultivate practices and routines that support balance and harmony. Take time for self-care, self-reflection, and spiritual nourishment alongside your daily activities. By seeking balance, you create a nurturing environment for the unity of your being to flourish.

9. Cultivating Self-Compassion: Cultivate self-compassion throughout your journey of unity and integration. Embrace the understanding that this is an ongoing process and that you are doing the best you can. Be gentle and patient with yourself, allowing for growth and learning along the way. Practice self-care and self-acceptance, honoring your journey with kindness and understanding.

10. Embracing Wholeness: Embrace the wholeness of your being, knowing that you are a beautiful and interconnected tapestry of body, mind, and spirit. Embrace all aspects of yourself—the light and the shadow, the strengths and the areas for growth. Embracing your wholeness allows you to experience a deep sense of unity, harmony, and integration within yourself.

By cultivating harmony and integration within the unity of your body, mind, and spirit, you embark on a transformative journey of self-discovery and growth. Honor your body, nurture mental clarity, and develop emotional intelligence. Connect with your spiritual essence and seek integration and alignment. Listen to your inner wisdom, seek balance, and cultivate self- compassion. Embrace the wholeness of your being and experience the profound unity that unfolds within you. As you cultivate harmony and integration, you create a fertile ground for well-being, balance, and fulfillment in your life.

Chapter 18
Multidimensional Perception of Time

Exploring the nature of time from a multidimensional perspective

Time, as we commonly understand it, is a linear concept that unfolds in a sequential manner. However, from a multidimensional perspective, time reveals itself as a complex and fluid phenomenon. In this chapter, we delve into the nature of time, exploring its multidimensional aspects and expanding our perception beyond its conventional constraints. By embracing a multidimensional perception of time, we open ourselves to a deeper understanding of the interconnectedness of past, present, and future.

1. Linear Time: Begin by acknowledging the conventional understanding of time as a linear progression from past to present to future. Recognize the practicality of this concept in organizing our daily lives and events. However, also realize that linear time is just one facet of a multidimensional perspective.

2. Non-Linear Time: Embrace the idea that time can be non-linear, with events and experiences not bound by a strict chronological order. Consider how memories can evoke emotions as vividly as if they were happening in the present moment. Reflect on how certain experiences may transcend time, leaving a lasting impact that transcends past, present, and future.

3. Time as a Human Construct: Contemplate the notion that time is a human construct, a framework created to make sense of our existence. Recognize that different cultures and civilizations have different ways of perceiving and

measuring time. Consider how time is influenced by societal norms, cultural traditions, and personal beliefs.

4. The Illusion of Time: Explore the idea that time may be an illusion, a construct of our human perception. Consider the relativity of time, as described by Einstein's theory of relativity. Reflect on how time can feel subjective and elastic, speeding up or slowing down depending on our experiences and states of consciousness.

5. Time as a Dimension: Embrace the concept that time is not only a linear progression but also a dimension in which we exist. Consider how time interacts with the other dimensions of space, creating a multidimensional reality. Reflect on how our perception of time can be influenced by our consciousness and awareness.

6. Simultaneous Existence: Contemplate the possibility of simultaneous existence, where all moments in time exist concurrently. Reflect on how different dimensions and realms may coexist, each with its own experience of time. Consider how past, present, and future may intertwine and influence one another.

7. Timelessness: Explore the notion of timelessness, where the constraints of time dissolve, and we tap into a timeless state of being. Reflect on moments of flow, when time seems to stand still and we are fully immersed in the present moment. Consider how practices such as meditation or creative pursuits can lead to experiences of timelessness.

8. Intuition and Time: Recognize the role of intuition in navigating the multidimensional nature of time. Reflect on how intuitive insights may transcend the linear concept of time, offering glimpses into future possibilities or deeper understanding of past events. Embrace the idea that intuition allows us to tap into a higher intelligence that transcends conventional time.

9. Embracing the Eternal Now: Embrace the eternal now, the timeless present moment where past and future merge. Cultivate mindfulness and presence, anchoring yourself in the here and now. Reflect on the power of the present moment, where all possibilities and potentials reside.

10. Transcending Limitations: Embrace the invitation to transcend the limitations of linear time and expand your perception of reality. Allow yourself to contemplate and explore the mysteries of time from a multidimensional perspective. Embrace the interconnectedness of past, present, and future, and the infinite possibilities that exist within the fabric of time.

By embracing a multidimensional perception of time, we open ourselves to a deeper understanding of the nature of existence. Reflect on the linear and non-linear aspects of time. Consider time as a human construct and explore the possibility of time as an illusion. Reflect on time as a dimension and contemplate the idea of simultaneous existence. Embrace timelessness and the eternal now. Cultivate intuition and embrace the power of the present moment. Transcend the limitations of linear time and embrace the expansive nature of multidimensional time. As you expand your perception of time, you open yourself to a deeper understanding of the interconnectedness of all things and the vast possibilities that exist within the fabric of time.

Opening up to nonlinear experiences of time

Time, as we commonly perceive it, flows in a linear fashion from past to present to future. However, the nature of time is far more intricate and multifaceted than our conventional understanding suggests. In this chapter, we delve into the concept of multidimensional time perception, inviting you to explore the possibilities of nonlinear experiences of time. By opening up to these expanded perceptions, we can tap into the richness and depth of our existence beyond the constraints of linear time.

1. Challenging Linear Time: Begin by challenging the notion of linear time as the sole framework for our experiences. Acknowledge that time can be experienced in various ways, free from the constraints of past, present, and future. Open yourself to the idea that time is not necessarily a linear progression but can be multidimensional and nonlinear.

2. Moments of Timelessness: Recall moments in your life when time seemed to dissolve, and you were completely immersed in the present moment. Reflect on experiences where time felt expansive and elusive, such as during deep states of meditation, creative flow, or moments of awe in nature. Embrace these moments as glimpses into the vastness of multidimensional time.

3. Synchronicities and Serendipities: Pay attention to synchronicities and serendipitous events in your life. Notice how they seem to defy the limitations of linear time, bringing together seemingly unrelated events or encounters. Reflect on the interconnectedness of these occurrences and the possibility that they are nudges from a multidimensional reality.

4. Past-Life Memories and Future Insights: Explore the idea that our consciousness may transcend time, allowing glimpses into past or future experiences. Reflect on any past-life memories or intuitive insights that you may have had. Consider how these experiences offer a broader

perspective on the nonlinearity of time and the continuity of consciousness across different temporal dimensions.

5. Dreams and Time Travel: Contemplate the role of dreams as gateways to nonlinear experiences of time. Explore how dreams can transport us to different temporal realities, allowing us to encounter people, places, and events from the past or future. Reflect on the possibility of consciousness navigating different dimensions of time during dream states.

6. Quantum Physics and Time: Delve into the realm of quantum physics, where time is viewed as a malleable construct. Explore concepts such as quantum entanglement, time dilation, and the observer effect. Reflect on how these principles challenge our conventional understanding of time and invite us to embrace a more expansive perception.

7. Flow States and Timelessness: Engage in activities that induce flow states, where you are fully immersed in the present moment and lose track of time. This could be pursuing a creative endeavor, engaging in a passion, or practicing mindfulness. Observe how these experiences offer a taste of timelessness and invite you to transcend linear time.

8. Embracing Present-Moment Awareness: Cultivate present-moment awareness as a doorway to nonlinear experiences of time. Practice mindfulness, grounding yourself in the present, and noticing the subtle nuances of each moment. By embracing the power of the present, you open yourself to the multidimensionality of time.

9. Trusting Intuition and Inner Guidance: Develop trust in your intuition and inner guidance as you navigate the realms beyond linear time. Pay attention to intuitive nudges and insights that transcend conventional logic. Allow your intuition to guide you in embracing nonlinear experiences and trusting the wisdom that arises from these realms.

10. Embracing the Mystery: Embrace the mystery of nonlinear time and the infinite possibilities it holds. Release the need for certainty and control, and instead, surrender to the unknown. Approach life with curiosity and openness,

allowing nonlinear experiences to enrich your journey of self-discovery and expansion.

By opening up to nonlinear experiences of time, we transcend the limitations of linear perception and access the vastness of multidimensional reality. Challenge the constraints of linear time and embrace moments of timelessness. Notice synchronicities and serendipities that transcend linear causality. Explore past-life memories, future insights, and the role of dreams in navigating different temporal dimensions. Delve into the principles of quantum physics and engage in activities that induce flow states. Cultivate present-moment awareness and trust your intuition. Embrace the mystery and allow nonlinear experiences to illuminate the beauty and depth of existence beyond linear time.

Chapter 19
The Evolutionary Path

Embracing the journey of personal and collective evolution

Life is a constant flow of growth and transformation, both at an individual and collective level. In this chapter, we delve into the concept of the evolutionary path, exploring the dynamic process of personal and collective evolution. By embracing this journey, we can cultivate a deeper understanding of our purpose, expand our consciousness, and contribute to the positive transformation of the world around us.

1. The Nature of Evolution: Reflect on the inherent nature of evolution, which involves continuous change, adaptation, and growth. Recognize that evolution is not limited to biological processes but encompasses every aspect of our existence, including our thoughts, beliefs, behaviors, and relationships. Embrace the idea that life is a perpetual journey of becoming.

2. Self-Reflection and Self-Awareness: Cultivate self-reflection and self- awareness as fundamental tools for personal evolution. Take time to examine your beliefs, values, and patterns of behavior. Explore your strengths, limitations, and areas for growth. Embrace a mindset of curiosity and openness to learn from your experiences. Self-reflection and self-awareness are catalysts for personal transformation.

3. Embracing Change: Embrace change as an integral part of the evolutionary path. Recognize that change can be uncomfortable and challenging, but it also holds the potential for growth and expansion. Cultivate a mindset that

welcomes change as an opportunity for learning, adaptation, and personal evolution. Embracing change allows you to flow with the natural rhythms of life.

4. Lifelong Learning: Embrace lifelong learning as a cornerstone of personal evolution. Cultivate a thirst for knowledge and seek opportunities to expand your understanding of the world and yourself. Engage in formal and informal education, explore new interests, and expose yourself to diverse perspectives. Lifelong learning nourishes intellectual, emotional, and spiritual growth.

5. Cultivating Resilience: Cultivate resilience as you navigate the evolutionary path. Recognize that challenges and setbacks are inherent to the journey of growth. Develop coping mechanisms and strategies to bounce back from adversity. Cultivate emotional and mental resilience, drawing upon inner strength, support systems, and a positive mindset. Resilience allows you to navigate obstacles and emerge stronger and wiser.

6. Relationship Dynamics: Recognize the impact of relationships on personal and collective evolution. Embrace connections that support your growth and inspire your highest potential. Surround yourself with individuals who challenge and uplift you, fostering an environment of mutual growth. Engage in meaningful dialogue, collaboration, and support within your relationships. The dynamics of relationships contribute to the collective evolutionary journey.

7. Compassion and Empathy: Cultivate compassion and empathy as essential qualities on the evolutionary path. Develop a deep understanding and appreciation for the interconnectedness of all beings. Extend kindness and support to others, recognizing that their journey is intertwined with yours. Practice active listening, seek to understand others' perspectives, and offer empathy in times of difficulty. Compassion and empathy nurture collective evolution.

8. Integration of Mind, Body, and Spirit: Strive for the integration of mind, body, and spirit on the evolutionary path. Cultivate practices that nourish your physical, mental,

and spiritual well-being. Engage in activities that promote physical health, such as exercise, nutrition, and rest. Develop mindfulness and cultivate a positive mindset for mental well-being. Connect with your spiritual essence through practices such as meditation, contemplation, or connection with nature. The integration of these aspects harmonizes your evolutionary journey.

9. Service and Contribution: Embrace the call to service and contribution as a vital aspect of personal and collective evolution. Identify ways to make a positive impact in your community and the world. Offer your skills, talents, and resources in service to others. Engage in activities that promote social justice, environmental sustainability, or the well- being of others. Service and contribution propel the evolution of humanity as a whole.

10. Embracing the Collective Evolution: Recognize that personal evolution is intricately linked to the collective evolution of humanity. Embrace a sense of interconnectedness with all beings, recognizing that our individual growth contributes to the evolution of the whole. Engage in collective endeavors, dialogue, and actions that promote positive change and transformation. Embrace the responsibility to co-create a more evolved and harmonious world.

By embracing the evolutionary path, we embark on a journey of personal and collective growth and transformation. Cultivate self-reflection and self- awareness, embrace change, and nurture resilience. Engage in lifelong learning and cultivate meaningful relationships. Cultivate compassion, integrate mind, body, and spirit, and embrace the call to service and contribution. Recognize the interconnectedness of personal and collective evolution. Embrace the responsibility to contribute to the positive evolution of humanity and the world. As you embrace the evolutionary path, you become an agent of positive change and contribute to the collective awakening and transformation of our global community.

Aligning with the greater cosmic plan

Within the vast tapestry of existence, there is a greater cosmic plan at play—a grand design that guides the evolution of all life. In this chapter, we explore the concept of aligning with this cosmic plan, understanding our unique role within it, and embracing the journey of personal and collective evolution in harmony with the greater whole. By aligning with the greater cosmic plan, we tap into a profound sense of purpose and contribute to the unfolding of a more enlightened and harmonious world.

1. Cosmic Order and Harmony: Reflect on the idea that the cosmos operates with an inherent order and harmony. Consider the intricate interplay of the stars, planets, and galaxies, and how they follow a divine rhythm. Embrace the understanding that this cosmic order extends to all aspects of creation, including ourselves. Aligning with the greater cosmic plan means attuning ourselves to this underlying harmony.

2. Divine Timing: Recognize the significance of divine timing in the evolutionary process. Reflect on how certain events and experiences align perfectly at the right moment, even if they may not make sense at first. Trust that there is a greater intelligence orchestrating the unfolding of life's journey. Embrace patience and surrender to the divine timing that guides your personal and collective evolution.

3. Synchronicity and Significance: Pay attention to synchronicities and meaningful coincidences in your life. Notice how certain events or encounters seem to be perfectly timed and hold profound significance. Embrace these synchronicities as signposts along your evolutionary path, guiding you towards alignment with the greater cosmic plan. Cultivate awareness and open yourself to the deeper meanings that these synchronicities hold.

4. Inner Guidance and Intuition: Cultivate a deep connection with your inner guidance and intuition. Recognize that this

inner wisdom is a conduit for aligning with the greater cosmic plan. Practice stillness, meditation, or contemplation to access this intuitive guidance. Trust the whispers of your heart and soul, as they hold the keys to your alignment and purpose.

5. Embracing Life's Lessons: Embrace the lessons that life presents to you on your evolutionary path. Recognize that challenges and obstacles are opportunities for growth and transformation. Approach difficulties with curiosity and openness, seeking the deeper lessons they hold. Embrace the understanding that every experience, both positive and negative, serves your evolution and alignment with the greater cosmic plan.

6. Co-Creation and Divine Partnership: Embrace the understanding that you are a co-creator in the unfolding of the greater cosmic plan. Recognize that you play a unique and valuable role in the grand design of existence. Cultivate a sense of partnership with the divine, allowing your actions and intentions to align with the higher purpose of creation. Embrace the responsibility to contribute to the greater good with love and compassion.

7. Trust and Surrender: Cultivate trust in the greater cosmic plan and surrender to its wisdom. Release the need for control and embrace the flow of life's unfolding. Trust that you are supported and guided on your evolutionary journey. Surrender to the divine intelligence that orchestrates the cosmic dance, knowing that it holds your highest good in its embrace.

8. Embodying Higher Frequencies: Align with the greater cosmic plan by embodying higher frequencies of consciousness. Cultivate qualities such as love, compassion, gratitude, and authenticity. Seek to elevate your vibrational state through practices such as meditation, self- reflection, and acts of kindness. Embodying these higher frequencies aligns you with the essence of the cosmic plan and contributes to its unfolding.

9. Unity Consciousness: Embrace the understanding of unity consciousness—the realization that we are all interconnected and part of a greater whole. Cultivate a deep sense of

compassion, empathy, and respect for all beings. Recognize that your evolution is intertwined with the evolution of all humanity and the Earth. Embrace the responsibility to contribute to the collective awakening and the realization of a more enlightened and harmonious world.

10. Embracing Divine Purpose: Embrace your divine purpose within the greater cosmic plan. Reflect on your unique gifts, talents, and passions. Seek to align your life's endeavors with this purpose, making choices that are in harmony with your soul's calling. Embrace the understanding that when you align with your divine purpose, you become a catalyst for the greater cosmic plan to unfold through you.

By aligning with the greater cosmic plan, we tap into a profound sense of purpose and contribute to the evolution of ourselves and the world. Embrace the order and harmony of the cosmos. Trust in divine timing and embrace synchronicities. Cultivate inner guidance and intuition. Embrace life's lessons and challenges. Recognize your role as a co-creator and cultivate trust and surrender. Embody higher frequencies and embrace unity consciousness. Embrace your divine purpose and contribute to the unfolding of the greater cosmic plan. As you align with this plan, you become an agent of profound transformation and participate in the co-creation of a more enlightened and harmonious world.

Chapter 20
Living as a 5D Being

Integrating the principles of the 5D Mind into everyday life

The journey of the 5D Mind has been an exploration of expanded consciousness, multidimensional perception, and alignment with the greater cosmic plan. In this final chapter, we focus on the practical application of these principles in our everyday lives. By integrating the principles of the 5D Mind, we can embody a higher state of being and create a more harmonious and fulfilling existence for ourselves and others.

1. Embracing Oneness: Embrace the understanding that we are all interconnected and part of a unified whole. Cultivate a sense of unity consciousness, extending love, compassion, and respect to all beings. Recognize the divinity within yourself and others, fostering an environment of harmony and acceptance.

2. Practicing Presence: Cultivate a state of present-moment awareness in your everyday life. Practice mindfulness and immerse yourself fully in the here and now. Release attachments to the past or future, and embrace the power of the present moment. By living in the present, you deepen your connection to the essence of life.

3. Aligning with Intuition: Trust your intuition as a guiding force in your decision-making process. Cultivate the practice of listening to your inner wisdom and allow it to lead you on your path. Trust the subtle whispers of intuition and let them guide your choices, actions, and interactions with others.

4. Engaging in Conscious Relationships: Nurture conscious and meaningful relationships based on authenticity, mutual respect, and growth. Embrace open and honest communication, deep listening, and empathy. Create a space where each person feels seen, heard, and valued. Engaging in conscious relationships supports the evolution of both individuals and the collective.

5. Cultivating Unconditional Love: Embody the essence of unconditional love in your thoughts, words, and actions. Extend love and compassion to yourself and others, free from judgment and conditions. Recognize that love is a transformative force that heals and unifies. Embracing unconditional love creates an environment of acceptance and harmony.

6. Embracing Co-Creation: Embrace your role as a conscious co-creator in shaping your reality. Align your thoughts, intentions, and actions with your highest vision and the greater cosmic plan. Engage in conscious manifestation, understanding that your thoughts and energy shape your experiences. Embrace the responsibility and power of co-creating a world aligned with love and harmony.

7. Living in Integrity: Align your thoughts, words, and actions with your inner truth. Live with integrity and authenticity, honoring your values and principles. Be true to yourself and cultivate a sense of congruence between your inner and outer world. By living in integrity, you become a beacon of light and inspiration for others.

8. Embracing Unity of Mind, Body, and Spirit: Recognize the importance of nurturing the unity of your mind, body, and spirit. Cultivate practices that support the well-being of each dimension. Engage in activities that promote physical health, mental clarity, and spiritual connection. Strive for balance and integration among these aspects of yourself, knowing that they are interwoven and contribute to your overall well-being.

9. Practicing Gratitude and Abundance: Cultivate a mindset of gratitude and abundance. Focus on the blessings and abundance in your life, expressing gratitude for both the big and small things. Shift your perspective from lack

to abundance, recognizing the infinite possibilities and potentials that exist. By practicing gratitude and embracing abundance, you attract more positivity and joy into your life.

10. Embracing Evolving Consciousness: Embrace the ongoing evolution of your consciousness as a lifelong journey. Remain open to new ideas, perspectives, and experiences. Seek personal growth and expansion through self-reflection, learning, and embracing challenges. Embrace the understanding that consciousness is ever-evolving, and you have the power to continuously grow and transform.

By integrating the principles of the 5D Mind into your everyday life, you embody a higher state of being and contribute to the creation of a more harmonious and fulfilling existence. Embrace oneness, practice presence, and align with intuition. Engage in conscious relationships, cultivate unconditional love, and embrace co-creation. Live in integrity, nurture the unity of mind, body, and spirit, and practice gratitude and abundance. Embrace evolving consciousness as a lifelong journey. As you integrate these principles, you become a beacon of light, radiating love, and contributing to the collective evolution of humanity and the planet. Live as a 5D being and inspire others to do the same.

Embracing the full potential of your multidimensional self

Throughout this journey of the 5D Mind, we have explored the depths of expanded consciousness, interconnectedness, and alignment with the cosmic plan. Now, in this final chapter, we focus on fully embracing the vast potential of your multidimensional self. By living as a 5D being, you unlock the power within you and create a life of fulfillment, purpose, and authentic expression.

1. Recognizing Your Multidimensional Nature: Embrace the understanding that you are a multidimensional being with layers of existence beyond the physical realm. Reflect on the interconnectedness of your physical, mental, emotional, and spiritual aspects. Embrace the recognition that you are more than the limitations of your physical body.

2. Connecting with Higher Realms: Cultivate a connection with higher realms of existence. Engage in practices such as meditation, prayer, or energy work to tap into higher states of consciousness. Seek guidance from your higher self, spiritual guides, or the divine. Allow yourself to explore the realms beyond the physical and embrace the wisdom and insights they offer.

3. Harmonizing Your Energies: Recognize the importance of harmonizing your energies—balancing your thoughts, emotions, and actions. Cultivate self-awareness and observe how your energy impacts your experiences and interactions. Practice energy healing techniques, such as Reiki or breathwork, to clear and balance your energetic field. Embrace the harmonious flow of energy within you.

4. Authentic Self-Expression: Embrace authentic self-expression as a cornerstone of living as a 5D being. Release the need for external validation and societal expectations. Express your true thoughts, feelings, and desires without

fear or judgment. Allow your unique voice and gifts to shine, contributing to the collective tapestry of creation.

5. Embodying Unconditional Love: Embody unconditional love in all aspects of your life. Extend love and compassion to yourself and others without limitations or conditions. Embrace forgiveness and let go of judgments. Recognize that love is the essence of your being and the transformative force that can heal and uplift all.

6. Embracing Unity Consciousness: Embrace the understanding of unity consciousness—that we are all interconnected and part of a greater whole. Cultivate empathy and compassion for all beings, recognizing that their well-being is intertwined with yours. Engage in acts of kindness and service, contributing to the collective evolution and well- being of humanity.

7. Expanding Awareness: Continually expand your awareness and consciousness. Seek knowledge and explore new ideas, perspectives, and experiences. Engage in practices that expand your consciousness, such as meditation, sacred rituals, or conscious travel. Embrace the understanding that there is always more to learn and discover about yourself and the universe.

8. Trusting Divine Guidance: Trust the guidance of the divine, your higher self, and the universe. Listen to the whispers of intuition and follow the signs and synchronicities that guide you along your path. Trust that you are supported and guided in every moment, even when the path seems uncertain. Surrender to the flow of divine guidance and allow it to lead you to your highest potential.

9. Embracing Co-Creation: Embrace your role as a conscious co-creator of your reality. Align your thoughts, intentions, and actions with your highest vision and the greater cosmic plan. Engage in conscious manifestation, knowing that you have the power to shape your experiences. Embrace the responsibility and joy of co-creating a life aligned with your soul's purpose.

10. Embracing Your Divine Essence: Finally, embrace your divine essence and your inherent divinity. Recognize that

you are a spark of the divine consciousness, uniquely expressing itself through you. Embrace your worthiness, power, and innate wisdom. Embody the fullness of your multidimensional self and radiate your divine light into the world.

By living as a 5D being, you embrace the full potential of your multidimensional self. Recognize your multidimensional nature and connect with higher realms. Harmonize your energies and express yourself authentically. Embody unconditional love and embrace unity consciousness. Expand your awareness and trust in divine guidance. Embrace co-creation and embody your divine essence. As you live as a 5D being, you inspire others to do the same, creating a world where love, unity, and conscious evolution thrive. Embrace your multidimensional self and live the extraordinary life that awaits you.

Expanding Love's Horizons

Introduction

Welcome to "5D MIND: Expanding Love's Horizons for Couples." This ebook is a comprehensive guide designed to help couples embark on a journey of love that transcends conventional boundaries and delves into the limitless dimensions of connection, compassion, and understanding.

In this fast-paced world, relationships often face challenges stemming from miscommunication, unresolved conflicts, and the absence of authentic connections. "5D MIND" advocates embracing five interconnected dimensions of love to create a fulfilling and transformative bond.

Conclusion

As you embrace the teachings of "5D MIND: Expanding Love's Horizons for Couples," you will embark on an extraordinary journey of love, exploring the vast and infinite dimensions that lie beyond the ordinary. Your relationship will flourish as you integrate physical, emotional, mental, spiritual, and energetic elements into your bond. Remember, the path to love is an ever-evolving process, and by nurturing these dimensions, your love will continue to grow and transcend beyond all boundaries. Embrace the 5D MIND and watch your relationship thrive like never before.

Chapter 1
Understanding the 5 Dimensions of Love

1.1
The Physical Dimension:
Sensuality and Intimacy

Love is a multi-faceted experience that encompasses various dimensions, each contributing to the richness and depth of the bond between two individuals. Among these dimensions, the physical aspect holds a special place, as it is the realm where sensuality and intimacy come to life. In this chapter, we explore the significance of the physical dimension and how it plays a pivotal role in nurturing love between couples.

1.1.1 The Importance of Physical Connection

The physical dimension of love involves the expression of affection, desire, and sensuality through touch, gestures, and intimate moments. It is through physical contact that we can convey our deepest emotions and desires without uttering a single word. A gentle touch, a warm embrace, or a lingering kiss can communicate love, care, and emotional support more profoundly than any spoken language.

Establishing a strong physical connection in a relationship helps build a sense of security, trust, and attachment. It fosters a deep bond between partners, creating a safe space where they can be vulnerable and authentic with one another. Physical affection also releases oxytocin, often referred to as the "love hormone," which further strengthens the emotional connection between couples.

1.1.2 Sensuality and Intimacy

Sensuality and intimacy are key components of the physical dimension of love. Sensuality involves engaging all the senses to heighten pleasure and create a deeper understanding of your partner's desires and needs. It goes beyond the mere physical act of touch to encompass a profound appreciation of your partner's body, mind, and soul.

Intimacy, on the other hand, refers to the emotional closeness and vulnerability shared between partners. It is a state of being deeply known and understood by your significant other, where walls are broken down, and true selves are revealed. Intimacy is the foundation upon which trust and emotional connection are built.

1.1.3 Nurturing the Physical Dimension

To cultivate a thriving physical dimension in your relationship, it is essential to prioritize and nurture sensuality and intimacy. Here are some practical tips to strengthen this aspect of your love:

1. **Create Intimate Rituals**: Set aside time to share intimate moments with your partner. It could be as simple as cuddling before sleep, sharing a romantic dinner, or going for a walk hand- in-hand. These small gestures contribute significantly to the physical and emotional bond.

2. **Communicate Your Desires**: Open and honest communication about your physical needs and desires is crucial. This ensures that both partners feel comfortable expressing themselves and understand each other's boundaries.

3. **Prioritize Physical Affection**: Physical touch is a powerful way to express love and care. Whether it's a hug, a kiss, or a gentle caress, make an effort to show affection daily.

4. **Be Present and Mindful**: During intimate moments, practice mindfulness and be fully present with your partner. This level of presence fosters a deeper connection and strengthens the emotional bond.

5. **Explore Sensuality Together**: Engage in activities that stimulate the senses together. It could be cooking a meal together, sharing a massage, or enjoying a romantic bath. These experiences create shared memories and strengthen the bond between partners.

6. **Embrace Spontaneity**: Surprise your partner with spontaneous gestures of affection and intimacy. Surprise dates, love notes, or unexpected kisses can keep the flame of passion alive.

In conclusion, the physical dimension of love is an integral part of a fulfilling and meaningful relationship. Sensuality and intimacy create a space for vulnerability, emotional closeness, and authentic connection between partners. By nurturing this aspect of your love, you lay the foundation for a strong, secure, and passionate bond that transcends time and challenges. Embrace the beauty of physical connection in your relationship and watch as it deepens and enriches your love journey.

1.2
The Emotional Dimension: Nurturing the Heart Connection

Love, at its core, is an emotional journey that transcends the boundaries of the physical world. The emotional dimension of love delves deep into the heart, where feelings of joy, compassion, vulnerability, and empathy intertwine to create a profound connection between two souls. In this chapter, we explore the significance of the emotional dimension and how nurturing the heart connection can lead to a truly fulfilling and lasting relationship.

1.2.1 The Power of Emotional Intimacy

Emotional intimacy is the cornerstone of the emotional dimension of love. It is the ability to be vulnerable and authentic with your partner, sharing your deepest fears, dreams, and emotions without fear of judgment. Emotional intimacy allows both partners to feel seen, heard, and understood, fostering a sense of emotional security and trust within the relationship.

When emotional intimacy thrives, couples can weather life's storms together, knowing that they have each other's unwavering support. It is through emotional connection that couples build a strong foundation for long-lasting love, creating a safe space to explore their individual growth and the growth of their relationship.

1.2.2 Nurturing Emotional Connection

To nurture the emotional dimension of love, couples must invest time and effort in cultivating emotional connection and intimacy. Here are some valuable practices to strengthen the heart connection:

1. **Practice Active Listening**: Be fully present and attentive when your partner communicates. Validate their feelings and show empathy. Understand that sometimes your partner may need to vent without seeking solutions, and your support can be enough.

2. Communicate with Openness and Honesty: Foster an environment of open communication where both partners feel comfortable expressing their feelings and thoughts. Avoid judgments and practice understanding, even if you disagree on certain matters.

3. Empathy and Compassion: Try to see the world from your partner's perspective. Put yourself in their shoes and acknowledge their emotions, even if you don't fully comprehend them. A compassionate approach helps bridge emotional gaps and strengthens the heart connection.

4. Share Your Dreams and Aspirations: Openly discuss your hopes, dreams, and goals with each other. Encourage and support one another in pursuing individual passions and aspirations, while also creating shared dreams as a couple.

5. Resolve Conflicts Mindfully: Conflicts are natural in any relationship, but how they are addressed matters. Engage in constructive discussions, focusing on finding solutions rather than blaming each other. Remember that you are a team working towards a common goal – a loving and harmonious relationship.

6. Express Gratitude and Appreciation: Regularly acknowledge and appreciate each other's efforts, affection, and presence in your life. Expressing gratitude strengthens emotional bonds and reinforces positive behavior.

1.2.3 The Journey of Emotional Growth

Embracing the emotional dimension of love is not a destination but a journey of growth and self-discovery. As you nurture your heart connection, you will witness the beauty of evolving together, deepening your love with each passing day.

Emotional connection allows you to create a love story that transcends time, becoming a source of strength during challenging times and a source of joy during moments of celebration. By nourishing the emotional dimension of love, you and your partner create a profound, lasting bond that enriches your lives and fills your hearts with immense love and compassion.

Conclusion

The emotional dimension of love is a sacred realm where hearts intertwine, and souls connect on a deeper level. Nurturing the heart connection is an ongoing process that requires emotional openness, vulnerability, and empathy. By embracing emotional intimacy, active listening, and compassionate communication, couples can create a foundation of love that withstands the tests of time and grows stronger with each passing moment. The emotional journey of growth and self-discovery is a beautiful path to embark upon together, leading to a love that enriches, empowers, and fulfills your hearts in ways unimaginable. Embrace the emotional dimension of love, and watch your relationship blossom into a beautiful symphony of hearts beating as one.

1.3
The Mental Dimension: Building a Strong Foundation of Communication

Love is not merely an emotional experience; it is also an intellectual journey that thrives on understanding, connection, and shared ideas. The mental dimension of love involves building a strong foundation of communication that fosters intellectual stimulation, mutual respect, and a deep understanding of one another's thoughts and perspectives.

In this chapter, we explore the significance of the mental dimension and how effective communication can strengthen the bond between couples.

1.3.1 The Role of Communication in Love

Communication is the lifeblood of any relationship, and in the context of love, it becomes the bridge that connects two souls. Effective communication is not just about speaking but also about actively listening and understanding. When partners communicate openly, honestly, and empathetically, they create an environment where they can freely express themselves without fear of judgment or rejection.

The mental dimension of love encompasses sharing ideas, beliefs, and values. It involves engaging in meaningful conversations that challenge and inspire growth, both individually and as a couple. Strong communication nurtures a sense of emotional intimacy, as partners feel secure in their ability to share their innermost thoughts and vulnerabilities.

1.3.2 The Power of Intellectual Stimulation

Intellectual stimulation plays a significant role in the mental dimension of love. Engaging in thought-provoking discussions, sharing knowledge, and learning from one another enhances the connection between partners. When couples challenge each other intellectually, they encourage personal growth and a deeper understanding of their unique identities.

Intellectual stimulation also keeps the relationship dynamic and interesting. As partners evolve intellectually, they create new avenues for shared experiences and mutual growth, fostering a love that continuously evolves and thrives.

1.3.3 Cultivating Effective Communication

To build a strong foundation of communication in your relationship, consider the following practices:

1. **Active Listening**: Be fully present and attentive when your partner speaks. Show genuine interest in their thoughts and feelings, and avoid interrupting or making assumptions. Active listening is the key to fostering understanding and empathy.

2. **Share Ideas and Interests**: Create opportunities to share your thoughts, ideas, and interests with your partner. Engage in conversations about topics you both find stimulating, and be open to exploring new perspectives and viewpoints.

3. **Respectful Disagreements**: It's natural for partners to have differing opinions on certain matters. Embrace disagreements as opportunities for growth and understanding. Approach discussions with respect and empathy, acknowledging that you both have unique experiences and viewpoints.

4. **Seek Common Ground**: While respecting individual differences, also seek common ground and shared values. Identifying areas of agreement strengthens your bond and provides a solid foundation for mutual growth.

5. **Be Mindful of Nonverbal Communication**: Communication isn't just about words; nonverbal cues, such as body language and facial expressions, also play a crucial role. Be aware of these cues and strive to communicate both verbally and nonverbally with love and understanding.

6. **Communicate Appreciation**: Express gratitude for your partner's contributions to the relationship, whether it's emotional support, intellectual stimulation, or everyday gestures of love. Acknowledging and valuing each other's efforts fosters a positive and loving environment.

1.3.4 Embracing Growth through Communication

The mental dimension of love invites partners to embrace growth, both individually and together, through open and honest communication. By cultivating effective communication and intellectual stimulation, couples create a strong foundation for understanding and mutual respect. This foundation not only enhances the emotional and intellectual connection but also empowers love to transcend challenges and obstacles.

Conclusion

The mental dimension of love is a powerful realm where intellectual stimulation and effective communication create a profound connection between partners. Building a strong foundation of communication allows couples to explore each other's thoughts, values, and interests, fostering a love that thrives on mutual understanding and growth. Embrace the art of communication and create a space where you and your partner can freely express yourselves, learn from each other, and evolve together intellectually. As you cultivate the mental dimension of love, you lay the groundwork for a love that is intellectually stimulating, emotionally fulfilling, and boundless in its capacity to grow and thrive.

1.4
The Spiritual Dimension: Transcending Together

Love is a transformative force that extends beyond the boundaries of the physical and emotional realms. The spiritual dimension of love delves into the essence of our being, connecting us to something greater than ourselves. It is a dimension that allows couples to transcend together, fostering a sense of unity, purpose, and higher consciousness. In this chapter, we explore the significance of the spiritual dimension in love and how couples can embark on a profound journey of spiritual growth.

1.4.1 The Essence of the Spiritual Dimension

The spiritual dimension of love acknowledges that there is a deeper purpose and meaning to our connections and experiences. It involves recognizing and nurturing the spiritual aspects within ourselves and our relationships. This dimension encompasses a belief in something greater, whether it be a higher power, universal energy, or the interconnectedness of all beings.

When couples embrace the spiritual dimension of love, they embark on a shared journey of growth, expansion, and awakening. It offers an opportunity to explore the depths of their souls, align their values and beliefs, and create a sense of unity that transcends the physical and emotional realms.

1.4.2 Cultivating Spiritual Connection

To cultivate the spiritual dimension in your relationship, consider the following practices:

1. **Shared Values and Beliefs**: Engage in open and honest discussions about your spiritual beliefs, values, and philosophies. Discover the common ground between your individual spiritual paths and seek ways to integrate them into your shared journey.

2. **Rituals and Practices**: Create rituals or engage in spiritual practices together. This could include meditation, prayer, gratitude exercises, or any other practices that resonate with your shared beliefs. By practicing together, you deepen your spiritual connection and create a sacred space within your relationship.

3. **Mindfulness and Presence**: Embrace the practice of mindfulness, being fully present in each moment with your partner. Cultivate a sense of deep connection and appreciation for the beauty and sacredness of your relationship.

4. **Seek Meaning and Growth**: Encourage each other's spiritual growth by seeking meaning and purpose in your lives together. Explore opportunities for personal and shared growth, whether it be through self-reflection, learning, or engaging in activities that nourish your souls.

5. **Service and Compassion**: Extend your spiritual connection beyond yourselves by engaging in acts of service and compassion. Seek ways to make a positive impact in the lives of others and the world around you, embodying the essence of love and unity.

1.4.3 The Power of Transcendence

The spiritual dimension of love offers the potential for transcendence - a state of being that transcends individual identities and merges into something greater. As couples nurture their spiritual connection, they tap into a wellspring of love, wisdom, and compassion that empowers them to navigate life's challenges with grace and resilience.

Transcendence allows couples to rise above petty conflicts, ego-driven desires, and attachments, embracing a love that is expansive, unconditional, and all-encompassing. It is through this transcendence that couples discover a deep sense of purpose, harmony, and interconnectedness with all of creation.

1.4.4 Embracing the Spiritual Journey

Embracing the spiritual dimension of love is an invitation to embark on a profound journey of self-discovery, connection, and growth. It is a journey that goes beyond the limitations of the physical world, offering couples a deeper understanding of themselves, each other, and the universe.

As you and your partner embrace the spiritual dimension of love, you tap into the infinite wellspring of wisdom, love, and unity. Your relationship becomes a sacred space where you co-create a reality that is grounded in compassion, purpose, and spiritual alignment.

Conclusion

The spiritual dimension of love invites couples to transcend together, nurturing a connection that is rooted in unity, purpose, and higher consciousness. By acknowledging and embracing the spiritual aspects within yourselves and your relationship, you embark on a journey of profound growth, wisdom, and interconnectedness.

As you cultivate your spiritual connection, you tap into a love that expands beyond the physical and emotional realms, guiding you towards a deeper understanding of your shared purpose and the interconnected nature of all beings. Embrace the spiritual dimension of love, and witness the transformative power it holds, allowing you and your partner to transcend the ordinary and embrace a love that is truly divine.

1.5
The Energetic Dimension: Harmonizing Your Vibrations

Love is more than a collection of emotions and thoughts; it is an energetic force that binds souls together. The energetic dimension of love delves into the subtle vibrations that emanate from each individual and the profound impact these energies have on a relationship. In this chapter, we explore the significance of the energetic dimension in love and how couples can harmonize their vibrations to create a deeper, more meaningful connection.

1.5.1 The Essence of Energetic Connection

The energetic dimension of love acknowledges that we are all energetic beings, constantly emitting vibrations that influence our interactions with others. These energetic vibrations shape the dynamics of a relationship, affecting the emotional, mental, and physical aspects of love.

When two individuals come together in love, their energies intermingle, creating a unique and dynamic energy field that is shared between them. This energetic connection goes beyond the visible and tangible, as it involves the exchange of subtle energies that are felt at a soul level.

1.5.2 Understanding Energetic Harmony

Energetic harmony in a relationship refers to the synchronization and alignment of both partners' vibrations. When couples are energetically attuned to each other, they experience a sense of flow, ease, and deep connection.

On the other hand, energetic disharmony can lead to emotional turmoil, misunderstandings, and a sense of distance. Negative energies, such as resentment, anger, or fear, can disrupt the flow of love and create barriers to intimacy.

1.5.3 Cultivating Energetic Connection

To cultivate the energetic dimension in your relationship and harmonize your vibrations, consider the following practices:

1. **Mindfulness and Self-awareness**: Practice mindfulness to become more aware of your own energetic state. Pay attention to your emotions and thoughts, as they are direct reflections of your energetic vibrations. By cultivating self-awareness, you can better understand how your energy impacts the relationship.

2. **Clearing and Releasing**: Regularly engage in practices that help release negative energies and emotional blockages. This may include meditation, energy healing, or journaling. Clearing and releasing allow you to approach your relationship with a lighter, more positive energy.

3. **Shared Activities**: Engage in activities that bring you joy and positive energy as a couple. Sharing uplifting experiences can create a harmonious energetic resonance between partners.

4. **Physical Touch and Affection**: Physical touch is a powerful way to exchange positive energy and reinforce the energetic connection. Hugs, cuddling, and intimate moments are not only emotionally comforting but also energetically enriching.

5. **Gratitude and Appreciation**: Expressing gratitude and appreciation for each other's presence and efforts fosters positive energy in the relationship. A grateful heart is naturally aligned with higher vibrations.

6. **Compassion and Forgiveness**: Cultivate compassion and practice forgiveness, both for yourself and your partner. Letting go of past resentments and grudges opens the way for energetic healing and renewal.

1.5.4 The Magic of Energetic Resonance

When couples consciously harmonize their vibrations, they experience a sense of unity and oneness that transcends the limitations of the physical world. Energetic resonance creates an energetic flow between partners, allowing love to flow effortlessly and unconditionally.

In a relationship of energetic resonance, both partners support each other's growth and well-being, creating a nurturing and empowering space. They become attuned to each other's needs, emotions, and desires, allowing them to respond to each other with sensitivity and understanding.

Conclusion

The energetic dimension of love introduces us to the subtle yet profound energies that underpin our connections with others. By cultivating energetic harmony, couples can experience a love that transcends the ordinary and reaches the realms of spiritual unity and oneness.

Harmonizing your vibrations in a relationship is an ongoing journey that involves self-awareness, mindfulness, and a commitment to cultivating positive energy. Embrace the power of energetic connection and allow the magic of resonance to enrich your love journey. As you harmonize your vibrations, you create a space for love to thrive, and your relationship becomes a sacred dance of energies in perfect harmony.

Chapter 2:
Embracing Your Authentic Selves

2.1
Self-Love: The Foundation of a
Fulfilling Relationship

Love begins within oneself. The journey of embracing your authentic self and cultivating self-love lays the foundation for a deeply fulfilling and meaningful relationship with a partner. In this chapter, we explore the significance of self-love and how it positively impacts the dynamics of a loving partnership.

2.1.1 The Essence of Self-Love

Self-love is the act of nurturing and valuing oneself unconditionally. It involves accepting all aspects of who you are - the strengths, weaknesses, vulnerabilities, and imperfections - with compassion and kindness. When you truly love yourself, you create a strong and resilient inner foundation, enabling you to love and relate to others in a healthy and fulfilling way.

2.1.2 Embracing Your Authentic Self

Embracing your authentic self involves being true to your values, beliefs, and desires. It means letting go of the need to conform to societal expectations or the expectations of others and embracing your unique essence. When you embrace your authentic self, you bring an unparalleled sense of genuineness and honesty to your relationship.

By being authentic, you open the door for a partner to love you for who you genuinely are, rather than a façade created to please or impress. Embracing your authentic self also empowers your partner to be authentic in return, creating an environment of mutual trust and vulnerability.

2.1.3 Cultivating Self-Love

Cultivating self-love is an ongoing journey of self-discovery and growth. Here are some practices to foster self-love in your life:

1. **Practice Self-Compassion**: Treat yourself with the same kindness and compassion you would offer to a loved one. Embrace your mistakes and imperfections, recognizing that they are a part of being human.

2. **Set Boundaries**: Learn to set healthy boundaries with yourself and others. Respect your needs and ensure they are honored, which ultimately fosters a sense of self-worth.

3. **Prioritize Self-Care**: Make time for self-care activities that nurture your mind, body, and soul. This could include engaging in hobbies, spending time in nature, or practicing mindfulness and meditation.

4. **Release Self-Judgment**: Let go of self-criticism and negative self- talk. Replace it with positive affirmations that reinforce your self- worth and capabilities.

5. **Celebrate Your Achievements**: Acknowledge your accomplishments, no matter how big or small. Celebrate your successes and give yourself credit for your efforts and growth.

6. **Surround Yourself with Supportive People**: Surround yourself with individuals who lift you up and support your journey of self- love and self-discovery.

2.1.4 Impact on Your Relationship

Embracing self-love has a profound impact on your relationship. When you love and accept yourself fully, you are better equipped to love your partner deeply and unconditionally. Your self-assuredness allows you to communicate your needs and desires authentically, fostering open and honest communication with your partner.

Moreover, when both partners embrace their authentic selves and practice self-love, they create a relationship built on mutual respect, understanding, and support. The acceptance of each other's uniqueness paves the way for a lasting and fulfilling partnership.

Conclusion

Self-love is the cornerstone of a fulfilling relationship. By embracing your authentic self and practicing self-love, you create a strong and resilient foundation for love to flourish. Your authentic expression fosters openness and vulnerability, allowing your partner to connect with the real you.

As you cultivate self-love, you not only enhance your relationship with yourself but also deepen the love you share with your partner. Remember that the journey of self-love is ongoing and transformative, and it sets the stage for a love that knows no bounds - a love that begins within and radiates out into the world. Embrace the power of self-love, and watch as your relationship blossoms into a beautiful reflection of authentic connection and genuine affection.

2.2
Empowering Vulnerability: Sharing Your Truths

In the journey of love, vulnerability is a profound and empowering act that opens the path to genuine connection and emotional intimacy. Embracing your authentic selves involves the courage to share your truths, fears, and vulnerabilities with your partner. In this chapter, we explore the significance of empowering vulnerability and how it strengthens the bond between couples.

2.2.1 The Power of Vulnerability

Vulnerability is the willingness to expose your innermost thoughts and emotions, even when it feels uncomfortable or scary. It is a powerful act of trust, allowing your partner to see the depths of your heart without judgment. When you embrace vulnerability, you invite your partner to do the same, creating a safe space for both of you to be authentic and real.

In moments of vulnerability, a deep emotional connection forms, as you allow your partner to witness your raw and genuine self. This connection fosters understanding, empathy, and a sense of closeness that can only be achieved through the courage to share your truths.

2.2.2 Overcoming Fear and Shame

The journey of embracing vulnerability can be hindered by fear and shame. Fear of rejection, judgment, or not being enough may hold you back from sharing your truths. Shame, which stems from past experiences or societal conditioning, can lead to feelings of inadequacy or unworthiness.

To empower vulnerability, it's essential to recognize and overcome these barriers. Embrace self-compassion and self-acceptance, acknowledging that vulnerability is not a weakness but a strength that deepens emotional connections.

2.2.3 Cultivating Empowering Vulnerability

To cultivate empowering vulnerability in your relationship, consider the following practices:

1. **Create a Safe Space**: Foster an environment of trust and non-judgment in your relationship. Assure your partner that they can be vulnerable without fear of ridicule or rejection.

2. **Practice Active Listening**: When your partner opens up, listen with an open heart and mind. Be fully present, offering empathy and understanding rather than trying to fix or solve their feelings.

3. **Share Your Truths Gradually**: Vulnerability doesn't have to be an all-or-nothing approach. Start by sharing small truths and gradually build up to more significant ones as trust deepens.

4. **Be Honest with Yourself**: Reflect on your fears and insecurities, and be honest with yourself about what is holding you back from being vulnerable. Acknowledge these feelings and work through them with self-compassion.

1. **Express Appreciation**: When your partner shows vulnerability, appreciate their courage and willingness to share. Let them know that you value their openness and that it strengthens your connection.

2.2.4 The Intimacy of Shared Vulnerability

Embracing vulnerability creates an intimate bond between partners. By sharing your truths, fears, and vulnerabilities, you allow your partner to see the depths of your soul, strengthening emotional intimacy and fostering a sense of emotional safety.

As you both embrace vulnerability, you create a safe haven for your relationship to thrive. Honest and open communication allows for deeper understanding, resolving conflicts, and navigating challenges together as a team.

Conclusion

Empowering vulnerability is an act of bravery that opens the door to genuine connection and emotional intimacy in a relationship. By embracing your authentic selves and sharing your truths with your partner, you create a safe space for both of you to be seen, heard, and understood.

Let go of fear and shame, and recognize that vulnerability is a strength that deepens your emotional bond. Cultivate empowering vulnerability by creating a safe space for openness, active listening, and mutual support.

As you both embrace vulnerability, you build a foundation of trust, compassion, and love that strengthens your relationship. The intimacy of shared vulnerability allows your love to grow and flourish in a way that transcends barriers and brings you closer together as you journey through life hand in hand.

2.3
Healing Past Wounds: Liberating Your Love

In the pursuit of love and connection, it is essential to recognize and address the wounds of the past that may hinder your ability to fully embrace your authentic selves. Healing past wounds is a transformative process that liberates your love, allowing you to build a relationship grounded in emotional freedom and understanding. In this chapter, we explore the significance of healing past wounds and how it liberates your love for a more profound and fulfilling partnership.

2.3.1 The Impact of Past Wounds on Love

Past wounds can cast shadows over your present relationships, influencing how you perceive yourself and others. Unresolved emotional pain from past experiences can manifest as fears, insecurities, or defensive behaviors that may impede your ability to authentically connect with your partner.

These wounds might stem from past relationships, childhood experiences, or unresolved traumas. When left unaddressed, they can create emotional barriers and limit your capacity to love and be loved fully.

2.3.2 Embracing the Healing Journey

Healing past wounds is a courageous and transformative journey of self- discovery and self-compassion. It requires facing the pain and emotions that have been buried, allowing yourself to grieve, forgive, and let go of the burdens that hold you back from experiencing love freely.

Embracing the healing journey involves:

1. **Self-Reflection**: Engage in self-reflection to identify and understand the root causes of your emotional wounds. Explore how these wounds might be affecting your current relationship dynamics.

2. **Seek Support**: Don't hesitate to seek professional support through therapy or counseling. A trained therapist

can provide guidance and a safe space for you to navigate your healing journey.

3. **Practice Forgiveness**: Forgive yourself and others for past hurts.

Forgiveness is a powerful act of releasing emotional baggage and liberating your heart to experience love without the weight of resentment.

4. **Practice Self-Compassion**: Be gentle with yourself throughout the healing process. Recognize that healing takes time and that it is okay to have moments of vulnerability and emotional release.

5. **Communicate with Your Partner**: Openly communicate with your partner about your healing journey. Share your experiences, fears, and hopes for the future, fostering a deeper understanding and connection.

2.3.3 Liberating Your Love

As you heal past wounds, you liberate your love from the shackles of the past. By addressing and transforming old emotional patterns, you create space for genuine love to flourish.

Liberating your love involves:

1. **Emotional Freedom**: Free yourself from the limitations imposed by past pain, allowing yourself to experience love with emotional freedom and vulnerability.

2. **Authentic Connection**: Healing past wounds enhances your ability to authentically connect with your partner. You can express your needs, desires, and emotions without fear of judgment or rejection.

3. **Empathy and Understanding**: As you heal, you develop a deeper sense of empathy and understanding for your partner's journey of healing as well. This mutual support strengthens your emotional bond.

4. **Embracing Imperfections**: Healing past wounds helps you accept imperfections in yourself and your partner. You recognize that healing is an ongoing process for both of you, fostering compassion and patience.

5. **Emotional Resilience**: Embracing the healing journey enhances emotional resilience, allowing you and your partner to navigate challenges together with greater strength and understanding.

2.3.4 Liberating Your Love Together

Couples who embark on individual healing journeys and support each other's growth experience a profound liberation of their love. Liberated love is not confined by past traumas or insecurities but is free to grow, evolve, and explore the depths of emotional intimacy.

As you both heal past wounds, you create a loving and empowering space that nurtures the authentic selves of each partner. Liberated love embraces vulnerability, compassion, and acceptance, fostering a relationship that flourishes in emotional freedom and unconditional understanding.

Conclusion

Healing past wounds is a transformative journey that liberates your love, allowing you to embrace your authentic selves and build a relationship grounded in emotional freedom and understanding. The process of healing involves self-reflection, forgiveness, self-compassion, and seeking support when needed.

By healing past wounds, you liberate your love from the chains of the past and create space for a deeply fulfilling and authentic connection with your partner. Embrace the healing journey together, and watch as your relationship blossoms into a beautiful symphony of emotional liberation and unconditional love.

Chapter 3
Mindful Communication Techniques

3.1
Active Listening: Hearing Beyond Words

Effective communication is the cornerstone of a thriving and harmonious relationship. Mindful communication techniques empower couples to truly connect and understand each other on a deeper level. Among these techniques, active listening stands out as a powerful tool that enables partners to hear beyond words and foster a genuine emotional connection. In this chapter, we explore the significance of active listening and how it enriches the fabric of love between partners.

3.1.1 The Essence of Active Listening

Active listening is more than just hearing the words that are spoken; it involves being fully present and attentive to the underlying emotions, needs, and desires conveyed by your partner. It is a practice of empathetic listening, seeking to understand not only the content but also the emotions and intentions behind the words.

When you engage in active listening, you show your partner that you value and respect their feelings and experiences. By being fully present in the moment, you create a safe space for open and authentic communication to take place.

3.1.2 The Art of Empathetic Connection

Empathy is at the heart of active listening. When you actively listen to your partner, you put yourself in their shoes, attempting to see the situation from their perspective. This empathetic connection fosters understanding, compassion, and emotional intimacy.

By acknowledging your partner's emotions and validating their experiences, you create a deeper sense of trust and emotional safety. Empathetic connection is a powerful force that enables partners to navigate conflicts with greater understanding and find resolutions that honor both perspectives.

3.1.3 Practicing Active Listening

To practice active listening in your relationship, consider the following techniques:

1. **Be Fully Present**: When your partner is speaking, put aside distractions and give them your undivided attention. Maintain eye contact and offer nonverbal cues, such as nodding, to show that you are engaged.

2. **Suspend Judgment**: Avoid interrupting or jumping to conclusions while your partner speaks. Suspend judgment and listen with an open mind and heart.

3. **Reflect and Validate**: Periodically reflect back on what your partner has said to ensure you understand their perspective correctly. Validate their emotions and experiences, even if you may not fully agree.

4. **Use Encouraging Responses**: Offer encouraging responses, such as "I understand," "Tell me more," or "How did that make you feel?" These phrases encourage your partner to share openly and honestly.

5. **Practice Mindfulness**: Cultivate mindfulness during conversations, being aware of your own emotions and reactions. Mindfulness helps you remain calm and centered during potentially emotional discussions.

6. **Ask Questions for Clarification**: If something is unclear, ask clarifying questions to gain a deeper understanding of your partner's thoughts and feelings.

3.1.4 Strengthening Emotional Intimacy

Active listening is a transformative practice that strengthens emotional intimacy between partners. By mindfully connecting with your partner's emotions and experiences, you create a deeper sense of emotional closeness.

Strengthening emotional intimacy through active listening involves:

1. **Building Trust**: When your partner feels heard and understood, trust deepens. This trust lays the groundwork for a strong and secure emotional bond.

2. **Enhancing Communication**: Active listening fosters effective communication. When both partners feel comfortable expressing themselves, conflicts can be resolved more harmoniously.

3. **Nurturing Empathy**: Empathetic listening nurtures empathy between partners. Understanding each other's emotions and perspectives leads to greater compassion and support.

4. **Deepening Connection**: Mindful communication through active listening nurtures a profound connection between partners. The emotional intimacy created paves the way for a love that is open, vulnerable, and enduring.

Conclusion

Active listening is a transformative communication technique that enhances the fabric of love between partners. By being fully present and empathetic, you create a safe space for open and authentic communication. As you engage in active listening, you strengthen emotional intimacy, build trust, and deepen your connection with your partner.

Practice the art of active listening with mindfulness and empathy, and watch as your relationship blossoms into a beautiful symphony of mutual understanding and love. Embrace the power of active listening and the profound impact it holds in nurturing a relationship built on genuine emotional connection and heartfelt communication.

3.2
Nonviolent Communication: Compassionate Dialogue

Communication is the lifeline of any relationship, and the way we communicate profoundly affects the quality of our connections. Nonviolent Communication (NVC), also known as Compassionate Communication, is a powerful technique that fosters empathy, understanding, and harmonious dialogue between partners. In this chapter, we delve into the significance of Nonviolent Communication and how it transforms communication dynamics within a loving relationship.

3.2.1 The Essence of Nonviolent Communication

Nonviolent Communication, developed by Marshall Rosenberg, is founded on the principles of empathy, honesty, and compassion. Its primary goal is to facilitate authentic and non-judgmental communication, allowing partners to express their feelings and needs openly while deeply understanding each other.

The core components of Nonviolent Communication are:

1. **Observations**: Describing specific, observable actions or situations without evaluation or judgment.

2. **Feelings**: Identifying and expressing emotions that arise in response to observations.

3. **Needs**: Articulating the underlying needs or values behind these emotions.

4. **Requests**: Making clear, positive requests to meet those needs.

By using this structure, NVC encourages partners to communicate in a way that leads to mutual understanding and the satisfaction of each other's needs.

3.2.2 Creating Emotional Safety

One of the main benefits of Nonviolent Communication is that it creates emotional safety within the relationship. When partners use NVC, they approach conversations with empathy and non-judgment, allowing each other to speak openly without fear of criticism or blame.

By expressing themselves in a nonviolent manner, partners foster an environment of trust and respect. Emotional safety nurtures vulnerability and openness, enabling both individuals to share their deepest feelings and needs freely.

3.2.3 Fostering Empathy and Understanding

Nonviolent Communication fosters empathy and understanding between partners. By focusing on feelings and needs rather than making accusations or assigning blame, individuals become more aware of their emotions and those of their partners.

The practice of empathetic listening helps partners develop a profound sense of compassion for each other's experiences and perspectives. This heightened understanding allows for conflicts to be approached with empathy, leading to more constructive and harmonious resolutions.

3.2.4 Transforming Conflict Resolution

Conflict is inevitable in any relationship, but how partners approach and resolve conflict determines the strength of their bond. Nonviolent Communication transforms conflict resolution by encouraging partners to express their feelings and needs without attacking or blaming each other.

By practicing compassionate dialogue, partners can listen to each other's concerns with an open heart and respond with understanding and empathy. NVC facilitates collaborative problem-solving and encourages creative solutions that honor the needs of both individuals.

3.2.5 The Power of Self-Reflection

Nonviolent Communication is not just about how partners interact with each other but also about self-reflection. It prompts individuals to identify and understand their feelings and needs, fostering emotional intelligence and self-awareness.

By practicing self-reflection, individuals become more in tune with their own emotions and triggers, leading to greater personal growth and emotional resilience. This, in turn, enhances their ability to communicate authentically and compassionately with their partners.

3.2.6 Embracing Nonviolent Communication in Everyday Life

To embrace Nonviolent Communication in your relationship, consider the following practices:

1. **Mindful Self-Awareness**: Observe your emotions and needs, especially during challenging moments, before communicating with your partner.

2. **Use "I" Statements**: Share your observations, feelings, and needs using "I" statements to avoid sounding accusatory or judgmental.

3. **Listen with Empathy**: When your partner speaks, be fully present and seek to understand their feelings and needs without interrupting or reacting defensively.

4. **Validate Emotions**: Acknowledge your partner's emotions and let them know you understand how they feel, even if you may not fully agree.

5. **Seek Common Ground**: Look for solutions that honor both partners' needs and find compromises that promote mutual satisfaction.

Conclusion

Nonviolent Communication, or Compassionate Dialogue, is a transformative technique that enhances communication dynamics within a loving relationship. By focusing on empathy, understanding, and authentic expression, partners create an environment of emotional safety and trust.

As couples embrace Nonviolent Communication, they foster a deep sense of compassion, open dialogue, and transformative conflict resolution. By using NVC in everyday life, partners cultivate emotional intelligence and self-awareness, empowering themselves to communicate with empathy and authenticity.

Embrace the power of Nonviolent Communication, and watch as your relationship flourishes into a harmonious symphony of compassionate dialogue, mutual understanding, and unconditional love.

3.3
Empathy and Understanding:
Walking in Each Other's Shoes

Empathy and understanding are the cornerstones of profound and meaningful connections in a loving relationship. Being able to step into your partner's shoes and truly comprehend their emotions, thoughts, and experiences strengthens the bond between you. In this chapter, we explore the significance of empathy and understanding in mindful communication and how they enrich your love journey.

3.3.1 The Power of Empathy

Empathy is the ability to understand and share the feelings of another person. When you practice empathy in your relationship, you show your partner that you genuinely care about their emotional well-being and that their experiences matter to you.

Empathy involves active listening, observing nonverbal cues, and being present in the moment. By immersing yourself in your partner's perspective, you create a deeper emotional connection and foster a safe space for vulnerability and open communication.

3.3.2 Cultivating Empathy

To cultivate empathy in your relationship, consider the following practices:

1. **Active Listening**: Give your partner your undivided attention when they share their feelings or experiences. Avoid distractions and be present in the moment.

2. **Nonverbal Communication**: Pay attention to your partner's body language and facial expressions, as they often convey emotions that words may not express fully.

3. **Validate Emotions**: Let your partner know that you understand and validate their emotions, even if you may not fully agree with their perspective.

4. **Seek to Understand**: Ask open-ended questions and seek clarification to gain a deeper understanding of your partner's thoughts and feelings.

5. **Be Non-Judgmental**: Refrain from judging or criticizing your partner's emotions or experiences. Create a safe space for them to express themselves without fear of judgment.

3.3.3 The Importance of Understanding

Understanding goes hand in hand with empathy. It involves comprehending your partner's thoughts, beliefs, and values and honoring their unique perspective. When you make an effort to understand your partner, you create a sense of validation and acceptance that is vital for emotional intimacy.

Understanding also involves being patient and compassionate, especially during challenging moments. It allows you to acknowledge that your partner's experiences and reactions are influenced by their past, and that everyone's journey is unique.

3.3.4 Practicing Perspective-Taking

To deepen understanding in your relationship, practice perspective-taking:

1. **Put Yourself in Their Shoes**: Imagine what it feels like to be in your partner's position and how their experiences have shaped their thoughts and emotions.

2. **Be Open-Minded**: Be willing to consider different viewpoints, even if they differ from your own. Embrace the diversity of perspectives in your relationship.

3. **Empathize with Their Needs**: Understand your partner's underlying needs and desires, and acknowledge that these needs may be different from your own.

4. **Offer Support and Compassion**: When your partner faces challenges, offer support and compassion. Show them that you stand by their side through thick and thin.

3.3.5 Strengthening Emotional Connection

Empathy and understanding strengthen the emotional connection between partners. When you walk in each other's shoes and truly comprehend one another, you create a profound sense of intimacy and trust.

This emotional connection allows you to be vulnerable and authentic with each other, knowing that your feelings and experiences are respected and valued. Empathy and understanding build a bridge that connects your hearts and souls, fostering a love that is enduring and unconditional.

Conclusion

Empathy and understanding are essential elements of mindful communication that enrich your love journey. By cultivating empathy, you create a safe space for your partner to share their emotions and experiences openly. Understanding allows you to honor each other's unique perspectives and journey.

Practice perspective-taking and be present in your partner's world, embracing their emotions, thoughts, and needs with compassion. As you walk in each other's shoes, you deepen your emotional connection, creating a relationship that is built on genuine empathy, understanding, and unconditional love.

Embrace the power of empathy and understanding, and watch as your relationship flourishes into a beautiful symphony of heartfelt connection and mutual appreciation.

Chapter 4
Reigniting Romance and Intimacy

4.1
Sparks of Passion: Nurturing Desire

Romance and intimacy are the fire that keeps love alive and flourishing. Over time, the initial spark of passion may dim, but with conscious effort and mindful nurturing, couples can reignite the flames of desire and cultivate a deeply passionate and intimate connection. In this chapter, we explore the significance of nurturing desire in a relationship and ways to reignite the sparks of passion.

4.1.1 Understanding Desire in a Long-Term Relationship

In the early stages of a relationship, desire often feels effortless and intense. As time goes by, the initial infatuation may wane, and daily routines, stress, or life's challenges can take center stage. However, this natural ebb and flow of desire doesn't mean that passion is lost forever.

Understanding that desire evolves and requires nurturing allows couples to take deliberate actions to keep the flame burning. Reigniting desire involves creating an environment of emotional and physical intimacy that encourages passion to thrive.

4.1.2 Prioritizing Emotional Connection

Emotional intimacy is the foundation upon which physical desire thrives. Connecting emotionally with your partner involves being open, vulnerable, and attentive to each other's feelings and needs. Make time for deep conversations, share your dreams, and actively listen to each other.

Expressing love and appreciation regularly reaffirms the emotional bond between you, fostering a sense of security and trust. Prioritizing emotional connection strengthens the pillars on which passion can build and flourish.

4.1.3 Embracing Novelty and Spontaneity

Novelty and spontaneity inject excitement into a relationship, igniting passion and desire. Embrace new experiences together, whether it's exploring new hobbies, going on spontaneous adventures, or surprising each other with thoughtful gestures.

Breaking away from routines and injecting spontaneity into your relationship keeps things fresh and invigorates the connection between you. Novelty triggers the brain's pleasure centers, creating a sense of excitement akin to the early days of courtship.

4.1.4 Cultivating Physical Intimacy

Physical intimacy is a vital aspect of desire in a romantic relationship. While it may evolve over time, it remains a powerful way to connect with your partner on a deep level.

Cultivate physical intimacy by:

1. **Touch and Affection**: Embrace the power of touch - holding hands, hugging, and kissing. Physical affection communicates love and desire nonverbally.

2. **Intimate Communication**: Discuss your desires, fantasies, and boundaries openly with each other. Honest communication builds trust and strengthens emotional and physical intimacy.

3. **Sensuality**: Engage in activities that heighten your senses and sensuality. This might include cooking together, dancing, or sharing a relaxing bath.

4. **Create Intimate Spaces**: Set the mood for intimacy by creating a space that feels romantic and inviting. Dim the lights, play soft music, and eliminate distractions.

4.1.5 Nurturing Self-Desire

Individual self-desire is an essential component of reigniting passion in a relationship. Nurturing your own passions, hobbies, and personal growth makes you a more vibrant and attractive partner.

When you feel good about yourself, you exude confidence and allure. By prioritizing self-care, pursuing your interests, and cultivating self-love, you become more receptive to intimacy and connection with your partner.

4.1.6 Quality Time Together

Make quality time for each other a priority. Schedule regular date nights or weekend getaways to reconnect and strengthen your emotional and physical bond.

During these special moments, be present and attentive to each other. Engage in activities that both of you enjoy and use this time to focus solely on each other.

4.1.7 Gratitude and Appreciation

Never underestimate the power of gratitude and appreciation in nurturing desire. Express your love and appreciation for your partner frequently. Let them know how much they mean to you and what you adore about them.

Feeling appreciated and valued creates a positive feedback loop that fuels desire and strengthens your emotional connection.

Conclusion

Nurturing desire in a relationship is a continuous journey of emotional and physical connection. By prioritizing emotional intimacy, embracing novelty and spontaneity, and cultivating physical closeness, you can reignite the sparks of passion that will keep your love flourishing.

Remember to nurture your individual passions and practice self-love, for these qualities make you a more magnetic and desirable partner. Engage in quality time together, express gratitude and appreciation, and never stop exploring new ways to deepen your connection.

As you consciously nurture desire in your relationship, you create a lasting and passionate love that withstands the tests of time. Embrace the power of passion, and watch as your love journey becomes a beautiful symphony of desire, intimacy, and boundless affection.

4.2
Reconnecting with Touch: The Power of Physical Affection

Physical affection is a powerful language of love that transcends words. Touch has the remarkable ability to reignite the flames of romance and intimacy in a relationship. In this chapter, we delve into the significance of physical affection and how it can rekindle the passion and emotional connection between partners.

4.2.1 The Importance of Physical Affection

Physical affection is a fundamental aspect of human connection. From the tender touch of a hand to the warm embrace of a hug, physical affection communicates love, care, and desire without the need for words.

In a long-term relationship, the power of touch can sometimes be overlooked or taken for granted. Reigniting romance and intimacy involves rediscovering the profound impact of physical affection and using it to deepen your emotional bond.

4.2.2 The Language of Love

Physical touch is one of the five love languages, as described by Dr. Gary Chapman. People express and receive love in different ways, and for some, physical touch is their primary love language.

By understanding and speaking your partner's love language, you can strengthen the emotional connection between you. For those whose love language is physical touch, affectionate gestures are vital in nourishing their emotional well-being and feeling cherished.

4.2.3 Embracing Different Forms of Physical Affection

Physical affection comes in various forms, and each one has its unique way of expressing love and intimacy. Some examples include:

1. **Hand Holding**: The simple act of holding hands communicates a sense of togetherness and emotional support.

2. **Hugs and Embraces**: Embracing each other warmly fosters feelings of security, comfort, and closeness.

3. **Kissing**: Kissing is an intimate and passionate expression of love that deepens emotional connection.

4. **Cuddling**: Cuddling or snuggling together enhances feelings of intimacy and promotes a sense of emotional bonding.

5. **Back Rubs and Massages**: Offering massages or gentle touches can be a soothing and loving gesture.

6. **Affectionate Touch During Daily Activities**: Express affection through small touches like brushing your partner's arm or giving them a gentle kiss before leaving for work.

4.2.4 The Healing Power of Physical Affection

Physical affection also has healing properties that soothe emotional wounds and reduce stress. In times of distress or sadness, holding your partner close and comforting them through touch communicates love and support.

Touch releases oxytocin, often referred to as the "love hormone," which promotes feelings of attachment and bonding. This chemical response deepens emotional intimacy and reinforces the emotional connection between partners.

4.2.5 Overcoming Barriers to Physical Affection

In some cases, barriers to physical affection may arise in a relationship. These barriers could be due to past traumas, emotional distance, or differences in love languages.

To overcome these barriers and reignite physical affection:

1. **Communicate Openly**: Talk to your partner about your feelings and desires for physical affection. Listen to their perspective and create a safe space for honest communication.

2. **Be Respectful**: Be mindful of your partner's comfort level and boundaries. Respect their need for personal space and physical touch preferences.

3. **Seek Professional Support**: If past traumas or emotional barriers are hindering physical affection, consider seeking professional guidance through couples therapy or individual counseling.

4. **Focus on Small Steps**: Reigniting physical affection doesn't have to happen all at once. Take small steps towards affectionate gestures, and gradually increase them as you both feel comfortable.

4.2.6 Making Physical Affection a Habit

Integrating physical affection into your daily life strengthens the emotional connection between partners. Make it a habit to express affection in various ways throughout the day, not just during intimate moments.

Remember that physical affection is not only reserved for romantic settings; it can be a part of your everyday interactions. From a loving peck on the cheek in the morning to a warm embrace before going to sleep, these gestures continuously nurture your love.

Conclusion

Physical affection is a powerful language of love that reignites romance and intimacy in a relationship. Embrace the significance of touch and rediscover its profound impact on your emotional connection.

By understanding and speaking each other's love language, you can tailor physical affection to your partner's needs and preferences. Overcome barriers and communicate openly about your feelings and desires for physical affection.

Make it a habit to express physical affection throughout your daily life, cultivating a deep sense of emotional bonding and intimacy. Embrace the power of touch, and watch as your relationship blossoms into a beautiful symphony of love, passion, and heartfelt connection.

4.3
Creating Intimate Rituals: Strengthening Your Bond

Intimacy thrives when couples invest time and effort into nurturing their emotional connection. Intimate rituals are special moments shared between partners that deepen their bond, reignite romance, and create lasting memories. In this chapter, we explore the significance of creating intimate rituals and how they strengthen the love and intimacy within a relationship.

4.3.1 Understanding Intimate Rituals

Intimate rituals are intentional actions, gestures, or activities that partners engage in regularly to express their love and affection. These rituals go beyond everyday interactions and hold a deeper meaning within the relationship.

Intimate rituals can take many forms, such as:

1. **Weekly Date Nights**: Setting aside one evening each week for a date night allows partners to reconnect and focus on each other without distractions.

2. **Morning or Bedtime Rituals**: Sharing morning coffee or tea together, or cuddling before bedtime, creates a sense of emotional closeness and sets a positive tone for the day.

3. **Writing Love Notes**: Leaving thoughtful notes or messages for each other reaffirms affection and reminds partners of their love.

4. **Cooking Together**: Preparing meals together fosters teamwork and shared experiences.

5. **Memory Journals**: Keeping a journal where you both write down special moments, dreams, or feelings allows you to reflect on your journey together.

4.3.2 The Power of Rituals

Intimate rituals hold great power in a relationship:

1. **Emotional Connection**: Regularly engaging in intimate rituals reinforces the emotional connection between partners. These rituals communicate love, commitment, and the importance of the relationship.

2. **Anticipation and Excitement**: The anticipation of upcoming rituals creates excitement and a sense of something special to look forward to.

3. **Relationship Stability**: Intimate rituals provide a sense of stability and consistency, especially during challenging times.

4. **Shared Meaning**: These rituals often hold personal significance to the couple, strengthening their unique bond and creating shared memories.

4.3.3 Customizing Your Intimate Rituals

Each couple is unique, and so are their intimate rituals. Customizing your rituals allows them to hold personal significance and meaning within your relationship.

Consider the following steps to create personalized intimate rituals:

1. **Reflect on Your Connection**: Think about what activities or gestures hold special meaning for both of you. Reflect on your journey as a couple and what moments have been the most cherished.

2. **Communicate and Collaborate**: Discuss your ideas and desires for intimate rituals with your partner. Collaborate on creating rituals that resonate with both of you.

3. **Keep It Simple**: Intimate rituals don't need to be extravagant.

Sometimes, the simplest gestures can hold the most profound meaning.

4. **Be Consistent**: Regularly engage in your chosen rituals to reinforce their significance and impact on your emotional connection.

4.3.4 Adapting to Life Changes

As life evolves, so too may your intimate rituals. Be open to adapting and evolving your rituals to fit the changes and challenges that come your way.

Life events such as moving to a new home, having children, or facing career changes may require adjustments to your rituals. Embrace these changes as opportunities to strengthen your bond further.

4.3.5 Expressing Gratitude

Gratitude is a key element in the power of intimate rituals. Express gratitude to your partner for their efforts in creating and participating in these rituals. Let them know how much you cherish these moments and how they enrich your relationship.

Gratitude reinforces the emotional connection and appreciation you have for each other, deepening the impact of your intimate rituals.

Conclusion

Creating intimate rituals is a beautiful and meaningful way to strengthen the bond between partners and reignite romance and intimacy. These intentional gestures and activities go beyond everyday interactions, expressing love and commitment in a unique and heartfelt manner.

Reflect on your connection, communicate with your partner, and collaborate on rituals that hold personal significance. Keep your rituals simple, consistent, and adaptable to the changes life brings. Express gratitude for these special moments, acknowledging their power in strengthening your emotional connection.

Embrace the beauty of intimate rituals, and watch as your love journey becomes a symphony of heartfelt gestures, cherished memories, and an enduring emotional bond that stands the test of time.

Chapter 5
Navigating Challenges and Conflicts

5.1
Conflict Resolution: Turning Struggles into Growth Opportunities

Conflict is a natural part of any relationship, and how couples navigate challenges can significantly impact the strength and resilience of their bond. Conflict resolution is a crucial skill that allows partners to transform struggles into opportunities for growth and understanding. In this chapter, we explore the significance of conflict resolution and how it fosters emotional connection and strengthens the foundation of love.

5.1.1 The Nature of Conflict

Conflict arises when two individuals with different perspectives, needs, and desires come together in a relationship. It is essential to understand that conflict does not imply a lack of love or compatibility; rather, it is a chance for growth and deeper understanding.

Resolving conflicts effectively requires open communication, empathy, and a willingness to work together to find solutions that honor both partners' feelings and needs.

5.1.2 Embracing Constructive Communication

Constructive communication is the cornerstone of effective conflict resolution. Instead of engaging in hurtful or defensive behaviors, partners should aim to communicate with respect, empathy, and openness.

Some tips for constructive communication during conflicts include:

1. **Use "I" Statements**: Express your feelings and needs using "I" statements to avoid sounding accusatory or attacking your partner.

2. **Active Listening**: Be fully present and actively listen to your partner's perspective without interrupting or jumping to conclusions.

3. **Stay Calm**: Maintain emotional regulation during conflicts. Take breaks if needed to avoid escalating emotions.

4. **Seek Understanding**: Ask clarifying questions to gain a deeper understanding of your partner's thoughts and feelings.

5. **Avoid Blame**: Instead of blaming each other, focus on the issue at hand and how both partners can work together to resolve it.

5.1.3 Finding Common Ground

Conflict resolution involves finding common ground and seeking win-win solutions. It requires a willingness to collaborate, compromise, and prioritize the well-being of the relationship over individual desires.

Seeking common ground may involve:

1. **Identifying Shared Goals**: Find areas where your goals align and work together to achieve them.

2. **Compromising**: Both partners may need to give a little to reach a resolution that satisfies both parties.

3. **Prioritizing the Relationship**: Keep in mind that maintaining a strong and healthy relationship is more important than "winning" an argument.

5.1.4 Nurturing Emotional Safety

Emotional safety is crucial during conflict resolution. Create a safe and non-judgmental space where both partners feel comfortable expressing their feelings and needs.

Avoid:

1. **Criticism and Contempt**: Avoid attacking or belittling your partner during conflicts.

2. **Defensiveness**: Refrain from being overly defensive, as it can hinder productive communication.

3. **Stonewalling**: Withdrawal or avoidance can escalate conflicts.

Stay engaged in the conversation.

Nurturing emotional safety encourages vulnerability, openness, and authentic communication, which are vital for resolving conflicts effectively.

5.1.5 Learning and Growing Together

Conflicts present an opportunity for personal growth and learning within the relationship. Embrace conflicts as chances to understand each other better, identify areas for improvement, and develop greater emotional intelligence.

Reflect on conflicts after they are resolved and discuss how both partners can grow individually and together. Use conflicts as stepping stones toward a deeper emotional connection and a more harmonious relationship.

5.1.6 Seeking Professional Support

Sometimes, conflicts may persist, or there may be deeper issues at play that require professional guidance. Seeking couples therapy or counseling can be a valuable step in navigating challenges and strengthening your bond.

A skilled therapist can provide a safe and impartial space for partners to explore their feelings and work through conflicts constructively.

Conclusion

Conflict resolution is a transformative skill that empowers couples to turn struggles into growth opportunities. Constructive communication, seeking common ground, and nurturing emotional safety are essential elements of effective conflict resolution.

Embrace conflicts as opportunities for learning and personal growth within the relationship. Prioritize the well-being of the partnership over individual desires and seek win-win solutions.

As you navigate challenges together, remember that conflict is a natural part of love's journey. By resolving conflicts with empathy, respect, and understanding, you foster a deeper emotional connection and lay the foundation for a love that endures and thrives. Embrace the power of conflict resolution, and watch as your relationship becomes a symphony of growth, compassion, and unwavering love.

5.2
Forgiveness and Letting Go: Freeing Your Love from Resentment

In the journey of love, challenges and conflicts are inevitable. At times, hurtful actions or misunderstandings can lead to resentment and emotional distance between partners. Forgiveness and letting go are powerful tools that enable couples to heal from past wounds, release negative emotions, and rebuild trust. In this chapter, we explore the significance of forgiveness and letting go in nurturing a love that is free from the weight of resentment.

5.2.1 The Healing Power of Forgiveness

Forgiveness is not condoning hurtful actions, but a conscious decision to release the negative emotions and resentment associated with them. It is a gift you give yourself and your partner, allowing both of you to move forward and heal.

Forgiveness is a healing process that involves:

1. **Accepting Emotions**: Acknowledge the pain and emotions resulting from the hurtful event. Allow yourself to feel these emotions without judgment.

2. **Empathy and Understanding**: Try to understand the reasons behind your partner's actions and their perspective at that moment. Empathy fosters compassion and a deeper connection.

3. **Compassion Toward Yourself**: Be compassionate toward yourself for any emotions you are experiencing. Allow yourself to heal at your own pace.

4. **Decision to Forgive**: Make a conscious decision to forgive your partner and release the resentment. Remember that forgiveness is an ongoing process.

5.2.2 Communicating Openly

To foster forgiveness and letting go, open communication is essential. Create a safe space to talk about the hurtful event, your feelings, and your desire for healing.

When discussing the issue:

1. **Use "I" Statements**: Express your emotions and needs using "I" statements to avoid sounding accusatory.

2. **Listen Actively**: Be present and actively listen to your partner's perspective without interrupting or being defensive.

3. **Be Honest and Vulnerable**: Share your feelings and experiences openly, allowing yourselves to be vulnerable with each other.

4. **Show Empathy**: Seek to understand your partner's emotions and experiences and show empathy in your responses.

5.2.3 Letting Go of Resentment

Letting go is a process of releasing the hold that resentment has on your emotions and thoughts. It involves:

1. **Self-Reflection**: Reflect on the impact of holding onto resentment and how it affects your emotional well-being and the relationship.

2. **Practicing Empathy**: Empathize with your partner's feelings and motivations, acknowledging that everyone makes mistakes.

3. **Focus on the Present and Future**: Letting go requires accepting that the past cannot be changed. Focus on building a better future together.

4. **Forgive Yourself**: If you are holding onto guilt or blame for your own actions, forgive yourself as part of the process.

5.2.4 Rebuilding Trust

Forgiveness and letting go are stepping stones to rebuilding trust in the relationship. Trust is a delicate element that takes time to rebuild after it has been damaged.

To rebuild trust:

1. **Be Consistent**: Show through your actions that you are committed to positive change and growth.

2. **Honesty and Transparency**: Be honest and transparent in your interactions and communications.

3. **Keep Promises**: Follow through on commitments and promises to demonstrate reliability.

4. **Seek Professional Support**: If rebuilding trust is challenging, consider seeking couples therapy or counseling for guidance.

5.2.5 Cultivating a New Beginning

Forgiveness and letting go pave the way for a new beginning in your relationship. As you release the weight of resentment, you create space for renewed emotional connection and intimacy.

Cultivate a new beginning by:

1. **Celebrating Growth**: Celebrate the progress you both make in healing and growing from the challenges you faced.

2. **Creating Positive Memories**: Engage in activities that create positive memories and experiences together.

3. **Expressing Gratitude**: Express gratitude for each other and the opportunity to rebuild and strengthen your love.

4. **Embracing Vulnerability**: Embrace vulnerability as you navigate the path to healing and renewed intimacy.

Conclusion

Forgiveness and letting go are transformative processes that free your love from the burden of resentment. Embrace the healing power of forgiveness and open communication to release negative emotions and rebuild trust.

Letting go allows you to focus on the present and create a new beginning, fostering a love that is stronger, more resilient, and free from the weight of past hurts.

As you navigate challenges and conflicts with forgiveness and letting go, watch as your relationship transforms into a symphony of healing, compassion, and a love that continues to grow and flourish. Embrace the power of forgiveness, and let your love soar to new heights of emotional connection and harmony.

5.3
Cultivating Patience and Tolerance: Embracing Imperfections

In every relationship, challenges and conflicts arise, often fueled by differences and imperfections. Cultivating patience and tolerance is a key to harmonious coexistence, allowing partners to embrace each other's flaws and grow together. In this chapter, we explore the significance of patience and tolerance in navigating challenges and conflicts, and how they lead to a love that embraces imperfections.

5.3.1 Understanding Patience and Tolerance

Patience is the ability to remain calm and composed in the face of difficulties or delays. Tolerance is the capacity to accept and respect differences, including imperfections, in oneself and one's partner.

In a relationship, patience and tolerance involve:

1. **Acceptance**: Recognizing that both partners are human and will have strengths and weaknesses.

2. **Compassion**: Showing understanding and empathy for each other's struggles and shortcomings.

3. **Flexibility**: Adapting to change and embracing growth as individuals and as a couple.

4. **Emotional Regulation**: Managing emotions during challenging moments and conflicts.

5.3.2 Embracing Imperfections

No one is perfect, and imperfections are a natural part of being human. Embracing imperfections in yourself and your partner fosters an atmosphere of acceptance and love.

Recognize that imperfections do not diminish love; rather, they make each partner unique and provide opportunities for growth and support.

5.3.3 Practicing Self-Awareness

Cultivating patience and tolerance starts with self-awareness. Be mindful of your own triggers, reactions, and emotions during challenging situations.

By understanding yourself better, you can respond to conflicts with more empathy and compassion, fostering a calmer and more constructive approach.

5.3.4 Communicating with Empathy

During conflicts and challenges, communicating with empathy is essential. Put yourself in your partner's shoes and seek to understand their perspective and emotions.

Approach discussions with an open mind and a genuine desire to listen and find common ground. Empathetic communication builds emotional connection and strengthens tolerance.

5.3.5 Setting Realistic Expectations

Setting realistic expectations for yourself and your partner can prevent unnecessary conflicts. Understand that neither of you is perfect, and disagreements are a normal part of any relationship.

Avoid placing unrealistic demands on your partner, and focus on supporting each other's growth and well-being.

5.3.6 Practicing Patience in Growth and Change

Personal growth and change take time, and patience is key in supporting each other's journey. Celebrate each other's progress and be patient during setbacks or challenging moments.Encourage each other to explore new interests and passions while being supportive and understanding.

5.3.7 Respecting Boundaries

Respecting each other's boundaries is crucial in fostering tolerance and understanding. Everyone has their limits and comfort zones.

Ensure you communicate and respect each other's boundaries to create a safe and nurturing space for growth and expression.

5.3.8 Celebrating Each Other's Uniqueness

Appreciate and celebrate each other's uniqueness. Embrace the diverse qualities, interests, and perspectives that make each partner special.

Celebrate your differences as opportunities for learning and expanding your own horizons.

Conclusion

Cultivating patience and tolerance is a transformative process that nurtures love and acceptance in a relationship. Embrace imperfections as a beautiful part of being human, and recognize that love grows when partners support and accept each other unconditionally.Practicing self- awareness, empathetic communication, and setting realistic expectations create an atmosphere of harmony and understanding.

As you navigate challenges and conflicts with patience and tolerance, watch as your love deepens into a symphony of acceptance, growth, and unconditional love. Embrace the power of patience and tolerance, and cherish a love that embraces imperfections and flourishes in the beauty of authenticity.

Chapter 6
Expanding Love through Adventure

6.1
Exploring New Horizons: Adventures Together

Adventure has a way of infusing love with excitement, joy, and lasting memories. Stepping out of your comfort zone and exploring new horizons together creates a sense of togetherness that strengthens the bond between partners. In this chapter, we explore the significance of adventure in expanding love and how shared experiences can enrich your relationship.

6.1.1 Embracing the Spirit of Adventure

Adventure doesn't always mean embarking on grand expeditions; it can be found in the simplest of experiences. Embracing the spirit of adventure involves being open to trying new things, exploring different places, and engaging in activities that create moments of joy and wonder.

Whether it's trying a new cuisine, taking a spontaneous road trip, or going on a hiking adventure, the shared thrill of exploring the unknown can deepen your emotional connection.

6.1.2 Creating Lasting Memories

Adventures together create lasting memories that you both cherish. These memories become threads in the tapestry of your relationship, strengthening the foundation of your love.

Remembering and reminiscing about these shared experiences fosters a sense of intimacy and nostalgia, reminding you both of the love and joy you have shared throughout your journey together.

6.1.3 Strengthening Emotional Bonds

Adventure brings partners closer emotionally. The shared experiences, challenges, and triumphs create a sense of camaraderie and support.

Through adventure, partners learn to trust and rely on each other, fostering emotional bonds that withstand the tests of time.

6.1.4 Fostering Growth and Learning

New experiences offer opportunities for personal growth and learning. Adventuring together allows partners to see each other in different contexts and explore aspects of their personalities that might not emerge in familiar settings.

The shared growth and learning experiences become a source of admiration and appreciation for one another.

6.1.5 Enhancing Communication and Teamwork

Adventures often require communication and teamwork to navigate challenges successfully. From reading maps on a road trip to collaborating on a new outdoor activity, partners learn to communicate effectively and work as a team.

These skills translate back into everyday life, enhancing overall communication and cooperation in the relationship.

6.1.6 Rekindling Romance

Adventure has a way of rekindling romance and passion in a relationship. The sense of excitement and the rush of adrenaline create an atmosphere of thrill and excitement, bringing partners closer together.

These moments of shared joy and excitement can lead to deeper emotional and physical intimacy.

6.1.7 Supporting Each Other's Dreams

Adventures often involve pursuing each other's dreams and interests. Supporting your partner in their pursuits shows love and dedication, while also creating opportunities for shared experiences.

By engaging in activities that are significant to each other, you reinforce your commitment to supporting and uplifting one another.

6.1.8 Creating a Love-Filled Life Story

Every adventure contributes to the narrative of your love story. Embrace the beauty of building a love-filled life story together.

From the spontaneous road trips to the daring endeavors, your love story becomes an epic journey that celebrates the essence of your partnership.

Conclusion

Embarking on adventures together expands your love and enriches your relationship with joy, growth, and lasting memories. Embrace the spirit of adventure and be open to trying new experiences that create moments of excitement and wonder.

As you explore new horizons together, remember that it's not the destination that matters most, but the journey you take together. The shared experiences, challenges, and joys become the foundation of a love that continues to thrive and flourish.

Embrace the power of adventure, and watch as your love journey transforms into a symphony of exploration, togetherness, and the celebration of a love that knows no bounds.

6.2
Traveling as a Couple: Uniting Through Shared Experiences

Traveling as a couple is an extraordinary adventure that allows partners to explore the world together, create lasting memories, and strengthen their emotional bond. It is a journey of discovery, growth, and unity through shared experiences. In this chapter, we delve into the significance of traveling as a couple and how it enriches love by fostering a deeper connection.

6.2.1 The Magic of Traveling Together

Traveling as a couple brings a sense of wonder and excitement. Stepping into new environments, cultures, and landscapes together allows partners to witness each other's curiosity and awe, creating a sense of admiration and shared enthusiasm.

The magic of travel lies not only in the destinations but also in the moments you create together along the way.

6.2.2 Building Lasting Memories

Travel experiences become cherished memories that strengthen the fabric of your relationship. From watching sunsets on distant shores to exploring historic landmarks hand in hand, these moments become threads in the tapestry of your love story.

As you revisit these memories together, you are reminded of the love and joy you have shared on your journeys.

6.2.3 Deepening Emotional Connection

Traveling as a couple provides a unique opportunity to deepen your emotional connection. In unfamiliar settings, you rely on each other for support, comfort, and shared decision-making.

The challenges and triumphs of travel foster emotional intimacy and trust, solidifying the bond between partners.

6.2.4 Embracing Shared Adventure

Traveling together is an adventure of a lifetime. The shared experiences of navigating new cities, trying local delicacies, and stepping out of your comfort zone create a strong sense of camaraderie.

These shared adventures become part of your love story, reminding you both of the incredible journey you've undertaken side by side.

6.2.5 Learning and Growing Together

Traveling as a couple is a journey of growth and learning. Experiencing different cultures and traditions exposes you to new perspectives and ways of life.

You learn more about each other as individuals and discover how you navigate challenges together, fostering personal and relationship growth.

6.2.6 Cultivating Flexibility and Patience

Traveling often involves unforeseen circumstances and unplanned moments. Cultivating flexibility and patience becomes essential in navigating these situations with grace and understanding.

By embracing the unexpected together, you learn to adapt, support each other, and communicate effectively, strengthening your partnership.

6.2.7 Rediscovering Romance

Traveling has a way of rekindling romance and passion in a relationship. The enchanting settings, shared adventures, and uninterrupted quality time create an atmosphere of love and intimacy.

Rediscover the joy of being in each other's company and revel in the romance that blossoms during your travels.

6.2.8 Strengthening Future Goals

Traveling together allows you to dream and plan for the future as a united team. Shared experiences often inspire new aspirations and dreams.

Discussing future travel plans and life goals strengthens your bond, as you envision a life full of adventure and love.

Conclusion

Traveling as a couple is a magical journey that unites partners through shared experiences, lasting memories, and emotional connections. Embrace the wonder and excitement of exploration, knowing that the true treasure lies not only in the destinations but in the togetherness you experience along the way.

As you navigate the world hand in hand, your love deepens into a symphony of admiration, support, and shared dreams. Embrace the power of traveling as a couple, and watch as your love story unfolds into an epic adventure of unity, growth, and love that knows no bounds.

6.3
Pursuing Common Interests: Deepening Your Connection

Shared interests have the power to weave threads of connection that strengthen the bond between partners. Pursuing common hobbies and passions is an adventure in itself, fostering emotional intimacy and a sense of togetherness. In this chapter, we explore the significance of pursuing common interests and how it deepens your connection, creating a love that is enriched by shared experiences.

6.3.1 The Joy of Shared Hobbies

Discovering and sharing hobbies that both partners are passionate about brings immense joy and fulfillment. Whether it's hiking, cooking, painting, or dancing, engaging in activities together creates a deeper emotional connection.

The shared joy of pursuing hobbies reinforces the idea that you are a team, supporting and encouraging each other's passions.

6.3.2 Growing Together

Pursuing common interests allows partners to grow together, both as individuals and as a couple. Learning and exploring new hobbies together leads to personal development and a sense of shared accomplishment.

As you master new skills or overcome challenges together, you strengthen your connection and create a reservoir of shared experiences.

6.3.3 Creating Quality Time

Life can be busy, and finding quality time to connect can be challenging. Pursuing common interests ensures that you dedicate time to each other regularly.

Engaging in hobbies together creates a natural environment for conversation and bonding, deepening your emotional intimacy.

6.3.4 Strengthening Communication

Shared interests provide fertile ground for open communication. Partners discuss ideas, collaborate on projects, and express their thoughts and feelings.

This exchange of ideas fosters effective communication, creating a safe space for openness and vulnerability.

6.3.5 Rediscovering Playfulness

As adults, we can sometimes forget the joy of playfulness and creativity. Pursuing common interests brings back the joy of play and allows partners to embrace their inner child.

Through laughter and shared fun, you nurture a light-hearted and playful atmosphere in your relationship.

6.3.6 Balancing Independence and Togetherness

Pursuing common interests is an excellent way to balance independence and togetherness in a relationship. You have the freedom to pursue individual hobbies while also enjoying shared activities.

This balance allows each partner to maintain their identity while deepening the connection they share.

6.3.7 Supporting Each Other's Passions

Supporting each other's passions creates a sense of emotional security and appreciation. Knowing that your partner encourages your interests fosters a deeper sense of love and trust.

By championing each other's pursuits, you nurture an environment of unconditional support and encouragement.

6.3.8 Celebrating Milestones Together

As you pursue common interests, you celebrate milestones and achievements hand in hand. From completing a challenging hike to finishing a joint project, you share a sense of pride and accomplishment.

These shared celebrations become markers of your growth and love journey together.

Conclusion

Pursuing common interests is an adventure that deepens the connection between partners. Embrace the joy of shared hobbies and passions, knowing that it is a pathway to emotional intimacy and a strengthened bond.

As you grow together, support each other's passions, and celebrate shared achievements, your love story transforms into a symphony of togetherness, growth, and shared happiness.

Embrace the power of pursuing common interests, and watch as your love journey flourishes with a richness of experiences, love, and understanding that knows no bounds.

Chapter 7
Spiritual Union and Transcendence

Love is not confined to the physical realm but has the power to transcend into the spiritual dimension, connecting partners on a profound level. In this chapter, we delve into the significance of spiritual union in a relationship and how it allows love to transcend boundaries, creating a deep sense of connection and transcendence.

7.1 Understanding Spiritual Union

Spiritual union is the alignment of two souls, where partners connect on a higher level beyond the material world. It involves shared beliefs, values, and a sense of purpose that unites them on a spiritual journey.

In a spiritually united relationship:

1. **Shared Values**: Partners align on fundamental values such as love, compassion, integrity, and empathy.

2. **Higher Purpose**: They find meaning and purpose in their lives, both individually and as a couple.

3. **Inner Growth**: The relationship becomes a catalyst for personal growth and spiritual evolution.

4. **Connectedness**: Partners feel deeply connected to each other, the world, and the universe.

7.2 Nurturing Spiritual Connection

Nurturing spiritual connection involves practices that foster a sense of unity and higher consciousness. These practices may include meditation, prayer, mindfulness, or engaging in acts of service and kindness.

By exploring spiritual practices together, partners deepen their connection and understanding of each other's spiritual journey.

7.3 Embracing Sacred Moments

In a spiritually united relationship, partners embrace sacred moments in their daily lives. These moments may include:

1. **Shared Reflections**: Taking time to reflect on their spiritual journey and sharing insights and learnings with each other.

2. **Gratitude Rituals**: Expressing gratitude for each other and the blessings they have in their lives.

3. **Nature Connection**: Connecting with nature and recognizing the divine in the world around them.

4. **Spiritual Celebrations**: Participating in spiritual celebrations or rituals that hold personal significance.

7.4 Transcending Ego and Conflict

Spiritual union allows partners to transcend ego-driven conflicts and seek resolution through love and understanding. They learn to respond with compassion and empathy, fostering harmony and growth in the relationship.

Through spiritual alignment, partners can view challenges as opportunities for growth and transformation.

7.5 Uniting Through Love and Acceptance

In spiritual union, partners unite through unconditional love and acceptance. They see the divine essence in each other, embracing each other's strengths and imperfections.

Spiritual love is free from judgment, allowing partners to feel safe and supported in their vulnerability.

7.6 The Journey of Transcendence

Spiritual union is an ever-evolving journey of transcendence. It involves:

1. **Surrender**: Letting go of attachment to the past and embracing the present moment.

2. **Trust**: Having faith in each other and the divine path they walk together.

3. **Unity of Souls**: Recognizing that they are connected on a soul level, beyond the physical form.

4. **Infinite Love**: Embracing the boundless love that transcends time and space.

7.7 Embodying Compassion

Compassion is at the core of spiritual union. Partners cultivate empathy and compassion not only for each other but for all beings.

By embodying compassion, they contribute to a more loving and harmonious world.

7.8 A Love Beyond Measure

In spiritual union, partners experience a love that transcends human measure. It is a love that knows no boundaries, one that elevates the relationship to a higher plane.

As they walk hand in hand on their spiritual journey, their love story becomes a symphony of transcendence, connection, and divine grace.

Conclusion

Spiritual union is a profound journey that elevates love to a transcendent level. By nurturing spiritual connection, embracing sacred moments, and embodying compassion, partners create a love that surpasses the limitations of the physical world.

Through spiritual alignment, love becomes a transformative force that unites souls, fostering growth, unity, and boundless love.

Embrace the power of spiritual union, and watch as your love story unfolds into an eternal symphony of transcendence and unity. May your shared journey be blessed with love, light, and the joy of knowing that your connection extends far beyond the horizon of time.

7.1
The Power of Shared Values and Beliefs

In a relationship, spiritual union goes beyond religious beliefs and delves into shared values, principles, and a sense of higher purpose. When partners align spiritually, they embark on a journey of transcendence that deepens their emotional connection and strengthens their love. In this chapter, we explore the significance of shared values and beliefs in fostering a spiritual union that elevates love to profound heights.

7.1.1 Understanding Spiritual Union

Spiritual union in a relationship is the convergence of shared values, beliefs, and a sense of connection to something greater than oneself. It can manifest in various ways, depending on each partner's spiritual or philosophical inclinations.

The spiritual dimension of a relationship involves:

1. **Shared Values**: Aligning on fundamental values such as compassion, empathy, honesty, and kindness.

2. **Higher Purpose**: Finding meaning and purpose in life, both individually and as a couple.

3. **Connection to the Universe:** Feeling interconnected with nature, humanity, and the world at large.

4. **Sense of Gratitude**: Cultivating gratitude for the blessings in life and expressing it to one another.

7.1.2 Deepening Emotional Connection

When partners share spiritual values and beliefs, they deepen their emotional connection. The understanding that both partners are working towards a common purpose brings a profound sense of unity and support.

Spiritual alignment enhances empathy and compassion, as partners view each other as souls on a shared journey.

7.1.3 Finding Comfort and Support

Spiritual union provides a source of comfort and support during challenging times. Believing in something greater than oneself can offer solace, strength, and hope in moments of difficulty.

Sharing spiritual practices, rituals, or meditations can also be comforting and uplifting for partners.

7.1.4 Embracing Mindfulness and Presence

Spiritual alignment encourages mindfulness and presence in the relationship. Being present with one another fosters active listening, understanding, and genuine engagement in conversations.

Embracing mindfulness allows partners to appreciate the beauty of the present moment and cherish their togetherness.

7.1.5 Encouraging Growth and Transformation

Shared spiritual values inspire personal growth and transformation. As partners evolve spiritually, they encourage each other to seek deeper truths, embrace change, and let go of limiting beliefs.

This shared journey of growth strengthens the bond between partners and fuels their love.

7.1.6 Nurturing Gratitude and Contentment

In a spiritually aligned relationship, partners cultivate gratitude for each other and their shared experiences. Gratitude fosters contentment and joy in the relationship, promoting an atmosphere of love and harmony.

Appreciating the blessings they have and expressing gratitude to one another enhances their emotional connection.

7.1.7 Connecting on a Deeper Level

Shared values and beliefs create a profound connection on an emotional and soulful level. Partners understand and accept each other's spiritual essence, which transcends external circumstances or challenges.

This deep connection brings a sense of peace and security to the relationship.

7.1.8 Supporting Each Other's Spiritual Journey

In a spiritually united relationship, partners support each other's individual spiritual journey. They encourage personal exploration and growth, respecting each other's unique path.

Supporting each other's spiritual quest strengthens their bond as they witness the growth and transformation in their partner.

Conclusion

Spiritual union is a powerful force that elevates love to new heights of connection and understanding. Embrace the significance of shared values, beliefs, and a sense of higher purpose, knowing that it is a journey of transcendence that brings profound meaning to your relationship.

As you deepen your emotional connection, find comfort and support in each other, and embrace mindfulness and gratitude, your love story becomes a symphony of spiritual unity and transcendent love.

Embrace the power of shared values and beliefs, and watch as your love transcends the boundaries of the material world, creating an enduring bond that resonates on a soulful level.

7.2
Meditative Practices: Connecting on a Soul Level

Meditation is a powerful tool that can deepen the spiritual union between partners, fostering a connection that transcends the physical realm. By engaging in meditative practices together, couples can create a sacred space for inner exploration, presence, and soulful connection. In this chapter, we explore the significance of meditative practices in cultivating spiritual union and connecting on a profound soul level.

7.2.1 The Essence of Meditation

Meditation is the practice of quieting the mind, cultivating mindfulness, and accessing a state of inner stillness. It provides an opportunity to turn inward, connect with one's inner self, and access deeper levels of consciousness.

Engaging in meditation as a couple allows partners to embark on a shared journey of self-discovery, presence, and spiritual connection.

7.2.2 Creating a Sacred Space

Establishing a sacred space for meditation is essential. Choose a quiet and comfortable area where you can sit together without distractions. Decorate the space with elements that promote tranquility, such as candles, incense, or meaningful objects.

By creating a dedicated space for meditation, you set the intention for deep connection and spiritual exploration.

7.2.3 Breathwork and Mindfulness

Breathwork is a foundational aspect of meditation. Together, focus on deep, conscious breathing, allowing the breath to anchor your awareness in the present moment.

Practice mindfulness by observing thoughts and emotions without judgment, bringing your attention back to the breath whenever the mind wanders.

7.2.4 Guided Meditations

Guided meditations can be a powerful tool for couples to explore their inner selves and connect on a soul level. Utilize guided meditations specifically designed for couples or choose ones that resonate with your shared intentions.

Guided meditations provide gentle guidance, allowing partners to synchronize their energy, emotions, and intentions during the meditation practice.

7.2.5 Loving-Kindness Meditation

Loving-kindness meditation, also known as metta meditation, is a practice that cultivates compassion and love. Together, focus on sending loving and kind intentions to yourselves, each other, loved ones, and all beings.

This practice deepens your capacity for empathy and strengthens the bond of love and understanding between partners.

7.2.6 Mantra Meditation

Mantra meditation involves the repetition of sacred sounds, words, or phrases to focus the mind and evoke specific qualities or energies. Choose a mantra that resonates with both partners, and synchronize your chanting or silent repetition.

Mantra meditation creates a harmonious vibrational field, fostering a deep sense of connection and spiritual union.

7.2.7 Silent Meditation

Silent meditation, without any specific focus or guidance, allows partners to enter into a space of pure presence and stillness. Sit in silence together, allowing your individual energies to merge and create a shared field of tranquility.

In the silence, partners can experience a profound sense of oneness and soulful connection.

7.2.8 Integration and Reflection

After the meditation practice, take a few moments to integrate the experience and reflect together. Share any insights, feelings, or sensations that arose during the practice.

Allow the meditative experience to deepen your understanding of each other and foster a sense of unity.

Conclusion

Meditative practices provide a sacred space for couples to connect on a soul level, transcending the physical and entering the realm of spiritual union. By engaging in meditative practices together, you create an environment of presence, inner exploration, and deep connection.

Through breathwork, mindfulness, guided meditations, loving-kindness practices, mantras, and silent meditation, couples cultivate a sense of oneness, empathy, and spiritual alignment.

Embrace the power of meditative practices, and watch as your love story unfolds into a symphony of spiritual union and transcendent connection. May your shared meditations guide you to the depths of your souls and strengthen the bond of love that transcends time and space.

7.3
Growing Together Spiritually: Ascending as One

In a spiritually united relationship, partners embark on a shared journey of growth, transformation, and higher consciousness. Growing together spiritually is a transformative process that allows love to transcend boundaries and ascend to higher realms. In this chapter, we explore the significance of growing together spiritually and how it leads to a profound sense of unity and transcendence.

7.3.1 Embracing Individual Spiritual Paths

Growing together spiritually does not mean following identical spiritual paths. Each partner may have unique beliefs, practices, and experiences.

Embrace the diversity in your spiritual journeys, and support each other's individual growth and exploration.

7.3.2 Sharing Spiritual Experiences

Share your spiritual experiences with each other openly and honestly. Communicate your insights, revelations, and moments of spiritual connection.

By sharing these experiences, you deepen your emotional bond and gain a deeper understanding of each other's inner world.

7.3.3 Practicing Mindful Communication

Mindful communication is essential in nurturing spiritual growth together. Be present and attentive when discussing spiritual matters.

Listen with an open heart and non-judgmental mind, allowing your partner to express themselves freely.

7.3.4 Exploring Spiritual Practices as a Couple

While respecting individual paths, explore spiritual practices you can do together. This may include meditation, prayer, or attending spiritual gatherings or workshops.

Engaging in shared practices strengthens the spiritual bond between partners.

7.3.5 Supporting Each Other's Evolution

As you grow spiritually, you may undergo shifts in beliefs and perceptions. Support each other through these changes, offering encouragement and understanding.

Allow your love to transcend any differences that may arise during your spiritual evolution.

7.3.6 Integrating Spirituality into Daily Life

Spiritual growth is not limited to formal practices; it extends into everyday life. Infuse your daily activities with mindfulness, compassion, and gratitude.

Let spirituality be a guiding force in how you relate to each other and the world around you.

7.3.7 Facing Challenges with Spiritual Wisdom

Spiritual growth equips you with wisdom to face challenges with grace and resilience. Instead of reacting impulsively, tap into your spiritual understanding to respond mindfully.

Approach conflicts and difficulties as opportunities for growth and learning.

7.3.8 Celebrating Milestones in Your Spiritual Journey

Celebrate significant milestones in your spiritual journey as a couple. These could be moments of profound insight, breakthroughs, or shifts in consciousness.

By celebrating together, you reinforce the unity of your spiritual paths.

7.3.9 Cultivating Unconditional Love

Above all, cultivate unconditional love in your spiritual growth. Love that transcends the ego, embraces imperfections, and cherishes the essence of each other's souls.

Let your love be a guiding light in your spiritual ascent.

Conclusion

Growing together spiritually is a sacred journey that binds partners on a profound level. Embrace the uniqueness of each other's spiritual paths, while cherishing the shared experiences that deepen your connection.

As you integrate spirituality into your daily lives, support each other's evolution, and face challenges with wisdom, your love story transcends the ordinary and ascends to a higher plane.

Embrace the transformative power of growing together spiritually, and watch as your love unfolds into an eternal symphony of unity, transcendence, and boundless love. May your shared spiritual journey lead you to new heights of consciousness and connection, uniting your souls in a divine dance of love and oneness.

Chapter 8
Energizing Your Love

8.1
Balancing Masculine and Feminine Energies: Embracing Your Dual Nature

In a harmonious and thriving relationship, partners embrace and balance both masculine and feminine energies within themselves. These energies represent different qualities and characteristics that contribute to the dynamic interplay of love. In this chapter, we explore the significance of balancing masculine and feminine energies in energizing your love and deepening your connection.

8.1.1 Understanding Masculine and Feminine Energies

Masculine energy embodies qualities such as strength, action, assertiveness, and analytical thinking. It represents the yang aspect of life - decisive and goal-oriented.

Feminine energy, on the other hand, embraces qualities like nurturing, receptivity, intuition, and empathy. It represents the yin aspect - nurturing and compassionate.

Both energies are inherent in every individual, regardless of gender, and play essential roles in maintaining balance and harmony.

8.1.2 Embracing the Duality Within

Each partner possesses both masculine and feminine energies. Embrace your dual nature and recognize the beauty of balancing these aspects within yourself.

Cultivate self-awareness to understand how each energy expresses itself in your thoughts, actions, and emotions.

8.1.3 Honoring Your Partner's Energies

In a relationship, honor and appreciate the unique balance of energies in your partner. Embrace their strengths, whether they align with traditional masculine or feminine qualities.

Recognize that both energies complement each other, enriching your connection.

8.1.4 Open Communication

Effective communication is crucial in understanding and balancing energies within the relationship. Share your thoughts and feelings about embracing both your masculine and feminine qualities.

Encourage open dialogue about how each partner's energies can be harmonized to enhance the relationship.

8.1.5 Creating Balance in Decision-Making

Harmonizing masculine and feminine energies in decision-making leads to a balanced outcome. Consider both rational and emotional aspects when making choices.

By integrating these energies, you tap into the wisdom of your heart and mind.

8.1.6 Expressing Vulnerability and Strength

Both vulnerability and strength are essential in a loving partnership. Allow yourself to be vulnerable with your partner, expressing your emotions and needs.

At the same time, embrace your inner strength, supporting your partner during challenging times.

8.1.7 Nurturing and Supporting

The feminine energy excels at nurturing and providing emotional support. Embrace these qualities, offering comfort and understanding to your partner.

At the same time, the masculine energy can support and protect, creating a sense of security and stability.

8.1.8 Harmonizing in Intimacy

Balancing masculine and feminine energies deepens intimacy in the relationship. Express vulnerability and tenderness while also fostering passion and desire.In this harmonious dance of energies, partners connect on a soulful level.

Conclusion

Balancing masculine and feminine energies in your relationship is a profound journey of self-discovery and unity. Embrace the dual nature within yourselves and honor the unique qualities each partner brings.

By harmonizing these energies, you create a dynamic and energized love that transcends limitations and fosters a deep sense of connection.

Celebrate the interplay of masculine and feminine energies, and watch as your love story unfolds into an eternal symphony of balance, passion, and oneness. May the union of your energies empower your love and inspire a harmonious dance of mutual understanding and appreciation.

8.2
Harnessing the Law of Attraction: Manifesting Love

The Law of Attraction is a powerful force that states that like attracts like. By harnessing this universal law, couples can manifest and energize their love, creating a profound and fulfilling connection. In this chapter, we explore the significance of the Law of Attraction in manifesting love and how you can use this energy to nurture and strengthen your relationship.

8.2.1 Understanding the Law of Attraction

The Law of Attraction asserts that the energy we emit through our thoughts, emotions, and beliefs attracts similar energies into our lives. Positive energy attracts positive experiences, while negative energy attracts negativity.

In the context of love, this law means that by cultivating love within yourselves and for each other, you magnetize more love into your relationship.

8.2.2 Embodying Love

To manifest love, both partners must first embody love within themselves. Cultivate self-love and self-compassion, nurturing a positive relationship with yourselves.

When you radiate love from within, you attract love into your life and your partnership.

8.2.3 Setting Clear Intentions

Setting clear intentions is a powerful way to manifest love. Define the qualities you seek in a loving relationship and visualize the kind of love you wish to experience with your partner.

Focusing on these intentions aligns your energy with the love you desire to attract.

8.2.4 Gratitude for Love

Expressing gratitude for the love you already share fortifies the Law of Attraction. Gratitude amplifies positive energy, attracting more reasons to be thankful for your partnership.

Regularly express appreciation for each other and the love you have.

8.2.5 Positive Affirmations

Use positive affirmations to reinforce your intentions and beliefs about love. Repeat affirmations such as "I am deserving of love," "Our love grows stronger every day," or "We attract joy and happiness into our relationship."

By affirming these positive beliefs, you create a magnet for love to flourish.

8.2.6 Visualization Exercises

Visualization is a potent tool in the Law of Attraction. Take time together to visualize your ideal relationship, focusing on the love, joy, and connection you share.

Engage your senses in this visualization, feeling the emotions and sensations as if your vision is already a reality.

8.2.7 Maintaining a Positive Outlook

Maintaining a positive outlook is vital in the process of manifesting love. Cultivate optimism and trust that the love you desire is on its way.

Believing in the abundance of love helps you attract more love into your relationship.

8.2.8 Releasing Limiting Beliefs

Identify and release any limiting beliefs or fears that may hinder the manifestation of love. Let go of thoughts that undermine your confidence in the power of love.

Replace these limiting beliefs with empowering and affirmative thoughts.

Conclusion

Harnessing the Law of Attraction is a transformative journey that allows partners to manifest and energize their love. By embodying love within yourselves, setting clear intentions, expressing gratitude, and using positive affirmations and visualization, you magnetize the love you desire into your relationship.

Maintain a positive outlook and release any limiting beliefs that may impede the flow of love. Embrace the power of the Law of Attraction, and watch as your love story unfolds into a symphony of abundance, connection, and fulfillment.

May the energies of love align and attract the depth of connection and happiness you both deserve. As you nurture the love within yourselves and for each other, may the universe respond with a resounding affirmation of love that knows no bounds.

8.3
Amplifying Love's Energy:
Cultivating Gratitude and Joy

Gratitude and joy are powerful catalysts that amplify the energy of love within a relationship. By cultivating these positive emotions, partners can infuse their love with a radiant and magnetic force. In this chapter, we explore the significance of gratitude and joy in energizing your love and how they create a harmonious and fulfilling connection.

8.3.1 The Power of Gratitude

Gratitude is a profound expression of appreciation and thankfulness. When partners cultivate gratitude within their relationship, they acknowledge the abundance of love and blessings they share.

By recognizing and acknowledging the goodness in each other and the relationship, love flourishes.

8.3.2 Counting Your Blessings

Take time to count your blessings together. Reflect on the positive aspects of your relationship, the love you share, and the happy moments you've experienced.

By counting your blessings, you shift your focus to the positive aspects of your love story.

8.3.3 Gratitude Practice

Incorporate a gratitude practice into your daily routine. Share with each other what you are grateful for, whether it's the little acts of kindness or the significant milestones you've achieved together.

Expressing gratitude regularly strengthens your emotional connection and fosters appreciation.

8.3.4 Joyful Moments

Find joy in the simple moments you spend together. Engage in activities that bring laughter, playfulness, and happiness into your relationship.

Celebrate the joy you experience in each other's company.

8.3.5 Cultivating Joyful Experiences

Seek out new experiences and adventures that bring joy to both partners. Whether it's trying new hobbies, exploring nature, or embarking on trips together, these shared experiences foster joy and connection.

Embrace the spirit of playfulness and curiosity in your relationship.

8.3.6 Emotional Alchemy

Transform negative emotions into opportunities for growth and connection. When challenges arise, approach them with a mindset of emotional alchemy, seeking the lesson or opportunity for deeper understanding.

By transmuting negativity into growth and love, you elevate your relationship.

8.3.7 Celebrating Each Other

Celebrate each other's achievements, big or small. Offer genuine support and encouragement when one of you accomplishes something meaningful.

Celebrating each other's successes strengthens the sense of partnership and mutual celebration.

8.3.8 A Heart Full of Gratitude and Joy

Cultivating gratitude and joy creates a heart full of love and positivity. As you nourish these emotions, your love's energy becomes magnetic and radiant.

A heart filled with gratitude and joy attracts more reasons to be thankful and joyful.

Conclusion

Gratitude and joy are like sunlight and water that nourish the garden of love in a relationship. By cultivating gratitude for each other and counting your blessings, you foster a deeper appreciation of the love you share.

Embrace joyful moments and seek out experiences that bring laughter and happiness, as they infuse your love with a playful and harmonious energy.

May gratitude and joy become guiding lights in your love journey, nurturing a profound sense of connection and fulfillment. As you amplify the energy of love through these positive emotions, may your relationship blossom into a symphony of gratitude, joy, and boundless love.

Navigating Human Connections

Introduction:

Welcome to the realm of the 5D Mind on Relationships, a guide that delves into the extraordinary journey of love and connection in higher dimensions. As we move beyond the constraints of the physical world, we explore the profound depths of consciousness and discover a new way of approaching relationships. This eBook aims to help you navigate the complexities of love, intimacy, and connection with a higher level of awareness, wisdom, and compassion.

Conclusion: Embracing the 5D Mind in Your Relationships

As we conclude this eBook, we reflect on the profound journey of exploring the 5D mind on relationships. By embracing higher dimensions of consciousness, love, and understanding, we create spaces of healing, unity, and growth. Our connections become soulful, elevating us to new levels of love and compassion. The 5D Mind on Relationships is not just a theory but a profound way of living that can bring harmony and fulfillment to your life and the lives of those you love.

Are you ready to embark on this transformative journey of love and connection? Let the 5D Mind guide you to deeper, more meaningful relationships that transcend the boundaries of time and space. Open your heart, expand your consciousness, and unlock the extraordinary potential that lies within your relationships in the higher dimensions.

Chapter 1
Understanding the 5D Mind

In a world where relationships often revolve around the tangible and the visible, the 5D Mind introduces us to an extraordinary way of perceiving and experiencing connections. As we step into the realm of higher dimensions, we transcend the boundaries of the physical and embark on a journey of profound understanding and enlightenment. Let us delve into the key elements of the 5D Mind and its impact on relationships.

1.1 Beyond the Three Dimensions

Traditionally, we perceive the world in three spatial dimensions - length, width, and height. However, the 5D Mind encourages us to look beyond these limitations and embrace additional dimensions that govern our existence. These dimensions are not physical locations but rather layers of reality that interact with each other. They offer us new perspectives on relationships and how they intertwine with the broader universe.

1.2 Energetic Interconnectedness

At the core of the 5D Mind lies the concept of energetic interconnectedness. We are all interconnected through the universal energy that flows within and around us. This understanding reveals that our thoughts, emotions, and intentions send ripples across the fabric of reality, influencing our connections with others. Recognizing this energetic exchange can help us navigate relationships with heightened awareness and sensitivity.

1.3 Consciousness Expansion

The journey towards the 5D Mind involves an expansion of consciousness. As we elevate our awareness, we begin to perceive relationships beyond the surface level. Our consciousness transcends the ego-driven desires and attachments, allowing us to see the essence of each being. This expansion fosters empathy, compassion, and a deeper understanding of the interconnectedness we share with all living entities.

1.4 Living in the Present

In the 5D Mind, the present moment holds significant importance. The past loses its grip on us, and the future becomes a canvas for co- creation. By living in the present, we free ourselves from the burdens of unresolved conflicts and old patterns, thus experiencing relationships in their purest form. Mindful presence allows us to cherish every interaction and create lasting memories in the tapestry of time.

1.5 Love as a Universal Force

Love takes on a transcendent meaning in the 5D realm. It is not just an emotion but a universal force that binds everything together. Love is the language of the 5D Mind, and through its expression, we harmonize with the cosmos. Relationships that thrive in higher dimensions are founded on unconditional love, radiating an authentic and **transformative energy that nurtures the souls of those involved.**

1.6 Embracing Oneness

As the 5D Mind expands our consciousness, we naturally embrace the concept of oneness. We recognize that we are all unique expressions of the same universal consciousness. In relationships, this understanding dissolves barriers, promotes inclusivity, and fosters a sense of belonging and support.

Conclusion:

Understanding the 5D Mind opens the gateway to a profound and transformative approach to relationships. By transcending the limitations of the three-dimensional world, we connect with others on a deeper level of energetic understanding and consciousness. Love becomes the driving force that unites us all, and our relationships become vessels for growth, healing, and enlightenment.

As we continue this journey of exploring the 5D Mind on Relationships, remember that this new perspective is not an escape from reality but an enhancement of it. Embrace the principles outlined in this chapter, and let them guide you towards more meaningful and fulfilling connections with others.

Chapter 2
Conscious Communication

Communication forms the very foundation of every relationship. In the realm of the 5D Mind, conscious communication takes center stage as a transformative tool for fostering deeper connections. In this chapter, we explore the art of communicating with presence, empathy, and authenticity, transcending mere words to convey emotions and intentions through energetic exchanges.

2.1 Listening with Presence

The first step in conscious communication is to listen with presence. In a world filled with distractions and constant stimuli, active listening becomes a rare and precious gift. When engaged in a conversation, focus your attention entirely on the other person, putting aside preconceptions and judgments. Be fully present in the moment, absorbing not just the words spoken, but also the emotions and energies underlying them.

2.2 Speaking from the Heart

Conscious communication involves speaking from the heart, bypassing the filters of the ego and societal conditioning. When you speak authentically, you express your true thoughts and feelings without fear of judgment. By communicating honestly, you invite openness and vulnerability in your relationships, creating an atmosphere of trust and intimacy.

2.3 Empathy and Compassion

The 5D Mind emphasizes the cultivation of empathy and compassion in communication. Seek to understand the perspectives of others, putting yourself in their shoes and acknowledging their emotions and experiences. Empathy bridges the gaps between individuals, fostering a sense of connection and shared understanding. Compassion, on the other hand, allows us to communicate with kindness and gentleness, even in challenging situations.

2.4 The Power of Non-Verbal Communication

In the realm of conscious communication, non-verbal cues speak louder than words. Pay attention to body language, eye contact, and subtle gestures when engaging with others. These cues convey emotions and intentions that may not be expressed verbally. Aligning your verbal and non-verbal communication enhances the clarity and sincerity of your interactions.

2.5 Honesty and Transparency

In higher dimensions of relationships, honesty and transparency are essential virtues. Avoid concealing your feelings or intentions to maintain harmony or avoid confrontation. Embrace vulnerability by sharing your authentic self with others. Honest communication builds trust and fosters an environment where both parties can express themselves freely without fear of judgment.

2.6 Transcending Language

Conscious communication in the 5D Mind transcends language barriers. As we open ourselves to energetic exchanges, telepathic communication may become more apparent. This form of communication goes beyond words and relies on sending and receiving intentions and emotions directly. Practicing telepathy in relationships can deepen connections and create a profound sense of unity.

2.7 Mindful Resolution of Conflict

Conflict is a natural part of any relationship, but in the 5D Mind, we approach it with mindfulness and grace. Instead of engaging in ego- driven arguments, seek to understand the root causes of conflict and explore solutions together. Embrace the idea that conflicts can be opportunities for growth and healing, leading to stronger bonds and mutual understanding.

Conclusion:

Conscious communication is a cornerstone of the 5D Mind on Relationships. By actively listening, speaking from the heart, and cultivating empathy and compassion, we create a space for deeper connections and authentic exchanges. Through non-verbal cues and telepathic understanding, we transcend the limitations of language, forging bonds that resonate on an energetic level.

As you continue your journey of conscious communication, remember that it is a skill that requires practice and patience. Embrace the beauty of vulnerability and honest expression, knowing that through this profound form of communication, your relationships will flourish and thrive in the higher dimensions of love and connection.

Chapter 3
Embracing Unity Consciousness

In the 5D Mind on Relationships, the concept of Unity Consciousness stands at the heart of transformative connections. It invites us to transcend the illusion of separateness and recognize the interconnectedness of all beings. Embracing Unity Consciousness in our relationships opens the gateway to a new way of loving, relating, and co- creating in harmony with the universe.

3.1 Dissolving the Illusion of Separateness

The illusion of separateness is deeply ingrained in our three- dimensional perspective. However, as we embrace Unity Consciousness, we begin to see beyond the surface appearances. We recognize that we are all expressions of the same universal consciousness, interconnected threads in the fabric of existence. By dissolving the illusion of separateness, we foster a sense of belonging and shared destiny in our relationships.

3.2 The Ego's Role in Unity Consciousness

The ego, driven by the need for self-preservation, often reinforces the belief in separation. However, in the 5D realm, the ego undergoes a transformation. Instead of asserting dominance and individuality, it learns to serve the higher self and the collective good. By taming the ego's desires, we cultivate humility and humility paves the way for Unity Consciousness to flourish in our connections.

3.3 Love as the Glue of Unity

Love becomes the adhesive that binds Unity Consciousness in relationships. This is not the love based on conditions or expectations but a love that recognizes the divinity in every being. Unconditional love allows us to see past flaws and imperfections, embracing others as they are and allowing our connections to thrive authentically.

3.4 Co-Creating in Harmony

Unity Consciousness opens the door to co-creating in harmony with the universe. Instead of pursuing individual goals, we align ourselves with the greater flow of life, seeking opportunities to contribute positively to the collective consciousness. In relationships, co-creation becomes a joint endeavor, where individuals support and uplift each other's spiritual growth and personal evolution.

3.5 Compassionate Understanding

Unity Consciousness brings forth compassionate understanding. We begin to perceive that each being is on their unique journey, shaped by their experiences and challenges. With this understanding, we approach others with empathy, supporting them without judgment or interference. Compassionate understanding strengthens bonds and creates a safe space for growth and transformation.

3.6 Transcending Duality

In Unity Consciousness, we move beyond the confines of duality - the idea of good versus bad, right versus wrong. We embrace the paradoxes of life and relationships, recognizing that opposing forces often complement each other. By transcending duality, we find balance and harmony in our connections, fostering an environment of acceptance and love.

3.7 Embracing Universal Oneness

Unity Consciousness ultimately leads us to embrace Universal Oneness. We realize that the same essence that flows within us is the very fabric of the universe. Our relationships become bridges to experience the interconnectedness of all life forms. This profound realization elevates our connections to a sacred and transformative level.

Conclusion:

Embracing Unity Consciousness in our relationships is a powerful and transformative journey. By dissolving the illusion of separateness, nurturing unconditional love, and co-creating in harmony, we elevate our connections to a higher plane of understanding and interconnectedness. In the realm of Unity Consciousness, compassion and empathy thrive, and we transcend the limitations of duality to embrace Universal Oneness.

As you embark on this path, remember that Unity Consciousness is not a destination but a continuous evolution of the soul. Nurture your relationships with love, understanding, and co-creation, and witness the magic of Unity Consciousness unfold in your life and the lives of those you connect with.

Chapter 4
Transcending Time and Space

In the 5D Mind on Relationships, we explore the extraordinary concept of transcending time and space in our connections with others. As we embrace higher dimensions of consciousness, we begin to perceive relationships as timeless and boundless, stretching beyond the limitations of physical existence. In this chapter, we delve into the profound nature of soul connections, soulmates, and the timeless essence of love.

4.1 Soul Connections

In the realm of 5D relationships, soul connections hold a significant place. These connections transcend the boundaries of time and space, originating from shared experiences and a deep soul-level resonance. Soul connections can manifest in various forms, from friendships to romantic partnerships, and they often carry a sense of familiarity and comfort that defies logical explanation.

4.2 Recognizing Soulmates

Soulmates are a particular type of soul connection that awakens us to a profound understanding of our journey through time and space. These individuals come into our lives to catalyze growth, healing, and spiritual evolution. Soulmates mirror our strengths and weaknesses, guiding us towards self-awareness and self-discovery. Recognizing and embracing soulmates in our relationships allows us to tap into the timeless wisdom and love they bring into our lives.

4.3 The Concept of Twin Flames

Twin flames represent the ultimate form of soul connection—a union of two souls that were once united as one in a higher dimension. When twin flames incarnate in separate bodies, their reunion becomes a powerful catalyst for spiritual awakening and growth. This connection transcends conventional relationships, as it involves an intense mirror- like dynamic that reflects both the light and shadow aspects of each individual's soul.

4.4 Love Beyond Lifetimes

The 5D Mind invites us to perceive love as a force that transcends lifetimes. We begin to recognize that the love shared between souls extends far beyond our current existence. This timeless love creates an eternal bond that can be felt and rekindled across different lifetimes. This understanding allows us to cherish our relationships in a more profound and enduring manner.

4.5 Lessons and Growth

As we transcend time and space in our relationships, we realize that every connection serves a purpose in our soul's evolution. Each relationship brings valuable lessons and opportunities for growth, whether through joy or challenges. Embracing these lessons with gratitude and an open heart accelerates our spiritual development and strengthens the bond with our soul connections.

4.6 Embracing Divine Timing

Transcending time involves embracing divine timing in our relationships. The universe orchestrates the meeting of souls, ensuring that we cross paths with those who contribute to our growth at the right moment. Trusting in divine timing allows us to surrender to the flow of life and appreciate the magic of serendipitous encounters.

4.7 Beyond the Physical: Energetic Connections

In the 5D realm, we understand that relationships are not solely dependent on physical proximity. Energetic connections exist independently of physical presence, and we can continue to nurture and communicate with our soul connections beyond the limitations of time and space. This awareness expands our capacity for love, compassion, and support in our connections.

Conclusion:

Transcending time and space in our relationships is an awe-inspiring journey that opens the door to the timeless nature of love and soul connections. By recognizing and embracing soulmates and twin flames, we deepen our understanding of our spiritual path. As we cherish the lessons and growth each connection brings, we realize that love exists beyond lifetimes, nurturing eternal bonds that span the cosmos.

Embrace the concept of divine timing and surrender to the flow of life, knowing that the universe orchestrates the meetings of souls in perfect harmony. As you navigate energetic connections and cherish the timeless essence of love, let your relationships become a gateway to the infinite beauty and wisdom of the 5D Mind.

Chapter 5
Healing and Growth

In the realm of the 5D Mind on Relationships, healing and growth become essential aspects of our journey. As we transcend the limitations of the physical world, we recognize that relationships provide fertile ground for personal and collective transformation. In this chapter, we delve into the power of self-awareness, self-love, forgiveness, and embracing challenges as catalysts for healing and growth.

5.1 The Path of Self-Awareness

Healing and growth in relationships begin with self-awareness. By turning our attention inward, we gain insight into our thoughts, emotions, and patterns of behavior. Self-awareness allows us to identify limiting beliefs, wounds, and unresolved traumas that may impact our relationships. Through introspection, we cultivate a deeper understanding of ourselves, paving the way for healing and personal evolution.

5.2 Embracing Self-Love

Self-love forms the foundation for healthy and fulfilling relationships. It involves accepting ourselves unconditionally, embracing our strengths and weaknesses, and nurturing our well-being. When we love ourselves deeply, we attract and cultivate relationships that mirror this love and respect. Self-love becomes a powerful catalyst for healing wounds and fostering growth in our connections.

5.3 The Power of Forgiveness

Forgiveness is a transformative force that frees us from the chains of resentment and pain. In the 5D Mind, forgiveness is not about condoning actions but about releasing emotional baggage and finding inner peace. By forgiving ourselves and others, we create space for healing and growth in our relationships. Forgiveness allows us to let go of past hurts and embrace the present moment with love and compassion.

5.4 Challenges as Catalysts for Growth

In the 5D realm, challenges and conflicts are viewed as opportunities for growth and evolution. Rather than avoiding or suppressing them, we embrace them as catalysts for deeper understanding and transformation. Challenges push us out of our comfort zones and invite us to expand our capacity for empathy, compassion, and resilience. Embracing challenges with an open heart allows us to cultivate stronger, more authentic connections.

5.5 Sacred Space for Healing

Creating a sacred space for healing within our relationships is crucial for growth. This space is characterized by trust, open communication, and vulnerability. It allows individuals to express their emotions, fears, and desires without judgment. Within this safe container, healing can occur, wounds can be acknowledged and transformed, and individuals can support each other's journey of self-discovery and healing.

5.6 Integration and Harmonization

Healing and growth in relationships involve integrating the lessons and experiences gained along the way. It is a process of harmonizing our personal growth with the evolution of our connections. Integration requires open and honest communication, mutual support, and a willingness to adapt and grow together. As we integrate our individual journeys, we create a foundation for a stronger and more fulfilling partnership.

5.7 Collective Healing and Expansion

In the 5D Mind, healing and growth extend beyond the individual level to encompass collective healing and expansion. As we heal ourselves, we contribute to the healing of the collective consciousness. Our relationships become vehicles for spreading love, compassion, and positive change in the world. By expanding our awareness and embracing unity, we actively participate in the evolution of humanity.

Conclusion:

Healing and growth are transformative elements within the 5D Mind on Relationships. By cultivating self-awareness, self-love, and forgiveness, we create a fertile ground for personal evolution. Challenges and conflicts become stepping stones for growth, and within the sacred space of our relationships, we support each other's healing journey. As we integrate our individual growth and expand into collective consciousness, we contribute to the healing and expansion of the world.

Embrace the path of healing and growth in your relationships, knowing that each step you take towards self-awareness and self-love benefits not only yourself but also the interconnected web of life. Let your relationships become catalysts for transformation, embodying the principles of the 5D Mind and spreading healing and growth far and wide.

Expanding Consciousness in the Digital Age

Introduction

Welcome to "5D MIND: Expanding Consciousness in the Digital Age." In this ebook, we will explore the concept of the 5D Mind and how it can help us navigate the complexities of our modern world. As we continue to evolve and adapt to the rapid advancements in technology, it becomes increasingly important to cultivate a multidimensional mindset that embraces both our humanity and the digital landscape we inhabit.

Conclusion

In "5D MIND: Expanding Consciousness in the Digital Age," we have embarked on a journey to integrate our humanity with the digital landscape, harnessing the power of the 5D Mind to navigate this rapidly evolving world. By cultivating awareness, embracing change, harnessing intuition, fostering connection, and leveraging technology consciously, we can expand our consciousness and create a harmonious coexistence between ourselves and the digital realm. Let us embrace the 5D Mind and embark on a transformative journey of self-discovery and collective evolution in the digital age.

Chapter 1
Understanding the 5D Mind

1.1
The Shift in Consciousness: Exploringthe concept of the 5D Mind and its relevance in the digital age

Introduction

The digital age has brought about profound shifts in the way we perceive and interact with the world around us. As technology continues to advance at an unprecedented pace, it has become crucial for us to adapt our consciousness to this new landscape. The concept of the 5D Mind offers a framework for understanding and navigating this shift in consciousness, enabling us to thrive in the digital age while remaining connected to our core humanity.

Defining the 5D Mind

The 5D Mind represents a multidimensional approach to consciousness that expands beyond the traditional three-dimensional perception of reality. It encompasses five key dimensions: awareness, interconnectedness, intuition, empathy, and adaptability. These dimensions provide a holistic perspective that empowers individuals to embrace the digital age while maintaining a strong sense of self and connection to others.

The Relevance of the 5D Mind in the Digital Age

In the digital age, we are bombarded with information, constant connectivity, and an increasing reliance on technology. This environment can sometimes leave us feeling overwhelmed, disconnected, and lacking authentic human connection. The 5D Mind offers a path to navigate these challenges by incorporating the following:

a) **Awareness** : Developing self-awareness in the digital age allows us to understand our thoughts, emotions, and actions in relation to the digital world. It helps us recognize the impact of technology on our well-being and make conscious choices about how we engage with it.

b) **Interconnectedness** : The digital age has connected us on a global scale, allowing us to interact with diverse cultures, ideas, and perspectives. The 5D Mind emphasizes the importance of recognizing our interconnectedness with all beings and fostering a sense of unity amidst the digital landscape.

c) **Intuition** : In a world overflowing with information, cultivating and trusting our intuition becomes essential. The 5D Mind encourages us to tap into our intuitive intelligence, enabling us to navigate the digital realm with discernment and make choices aligned with our authentic selves.

d) **Empathy** : The digital age has provided us with platforms to connect, but it also poses challenges to genuine human connection. The 5D Mind emphasizes empathy as a key element in relating to others and building meaningful relationships, both online and offline.

e) **Adaptability** : The rapid pace of technological advancements requires us to be adaptable and open to change. The 5D Mind fosters a mindset that embraces change and allows us to leverage technology as a tool for personal and collective growth.

Conclusion

Understanding the 5D Mind is essential for thriving in the digital age. By embracing the dimensions of awareness, interconnectedness, intuition, empathy, and adaptability, we can navigate the complexities of the digital landscape while remaining anchored in our humanity. This shift in consciousness empowers us to make conscious choices about our engagement with technology, nurture meaningful connections, and cultivate a sense of harmony and balance in our lives. In the following chapters, we will delve deeper into each dimension of the 5D Mind, exploring practical strategies and techniques to integrate them into our daily lives.

1.2
Dimensions of Consciousness: A deeper exploration of the five dimensions of the 5D Mind and their interconnectedness

Introduction

In Chapter 1, we introduced the concept of the 5D Mind and its relevance in the digital age. Now, let us delve deeper into the five dimensions that comprise the 5D Mind: awareness, interconnectedness, intuition, empathy, and adaptability. These dimensions are interconnected and synergistic, creating a holistic framework for expanding consciousness and navigating the complexities of the modern world.

Awareness

Awareness forms the foundation of the 5D Mind. It involves being fully present, observing our thoughts, emotions, and actions without judgment. In the digital age, where distractions abound, cultivating awareness helps us disengage from autopilot and make conscious choices about our interactions with technology. Through practices such as mindfulness and meditation, we can develop a heightened sense of self-awareness and navigate the digital realm with intention and clarity.

Interconnectedness

Interconnectedness recognizes that we are all part of a larger whole. In the digital age, the boundaries that once separated us are becoming increasingly blurred. The internet has connected us globally, allowing for the exchange of ideas, cultures, and perspectives. Embracing interconnectedness means acknowledging the impact our actions have on others and the planet. It encourages us to cultivate compassion, empathy, and a sense of unity amidst the diversity, fostering a collective consciousness that transcends geographical and cultural boundaries.

Intuition

Intuition is our inner guidance system, an innate intelligence that transcends logical reasoning. In the digital age, where information overload is prevalent, tapping into our intuition becomes paramount. Honoring our intuition allows us to discern what is relevant and aligns with our values and authentic selves. Practices such as meditation, journaling, and reflective contemplation can help us develop a deeper connection with our intuition, enabling us to make decisions that are in harmony with our highest good.

Empathy

Empathy is the ability to understand and share the feelings of others. In the digital realm, where communication often occurs through screens and text, it is essential to foster empathy to maintain genuine human connection. Empathy involves active listening, seeking to understand perspectives different from our own, and cultivating compassion for others' experiences. By empathizing with others, we foster a sense of connection and promote a culture of kindness and understanding in the digital space.

Adaptability

Adaptability is the capacity to embrace change and respond flexibly to new circumstances. In the digital age, where technology is constantly evolving, cultivating adaptability is crucial. It involves being open-minded, willing to learn, and embracing new technologies as tools for growth and transformation. By embracing adaptability, we can navigate the rapid changes of the digital world with resilience and grace, leveraging emerging opportunities for personal and collective evolution

Conclusion

The dimensions of awareness, interconnectedness, intuition, empathy, and adaptability form the interconnected fabric of the 5D Mind. By embracing these dimensions, we expand our consciousness and develop a holistic approach to navigating the digital age. Recognizing the interplay between these dimensions allows us to cultivate a balanced and harmonious relationship with technology, fostering meaningful connections, and contributing to our personal growth and the betterment of the world around us. In the upcoming chapters, we will explore practical techniques and strategies to integrate these dimensions into our daily lives, empowering to embody the 5D Mind and thrive in the digital age.

1.3
The Intersection of Humanity and Technology: Recognizing the symbiotic relationship between human consciousness and technological advancements

Introduction

In Chapter 1, we explored the dimensions of the 5D Mind and their significance in our lives. Now, let us delve into the intersection of humanity and technology, recognizing the dynamic and symbiotic relationship between human consciousness and technological advancements. As we navigate the digital age, it is essential to understand how technology impacts our consciousness and how our consciousness shapes the development and use of technology.

The Influence of Technology on Consciousness

Technology has profoundly transformed the way we live, work, and interact with the world. It has expanded our access to information, facilitated global communication, and provided new avenues for creativity and self-expression. However, it has also presented challenges, such as information overload, digital distractions, and a potential disconnection from authentic human connection.

1.1. Information Overload and Digital Distractions

The digital age inundates us with vast amounts of information, constantly vying for our attention. This overload can lead to mental and emotional fatigue, reduced focus, and a fragmented sense of self. It is crucial to cultivate awareness and discernment to navigate through this sea of information, filtering what is valuable and aligns with our well-being.

1.2 Disconnection and Authentic Human Connection

While technology has connected us in unprecedented ways, it can also create a sense of disconnection. Online interactions, while convenient, lack the depth and nuances of face-to-face communication. It is essential to balance our digital engagement with intentional efforts to foster authentic human connection, empathy, and meaningful relationships.

The Impact of Consciousness on Technology

Conversely, human consciousness plays a significant role in shaping the development and use of technology. Our desires, aspirations, and values shape the trajectory of technological advancements. It is crucial to recognize our responsibility in utilizing technology consciously and ethically, aligning it with our collective well-being and sustainable future.

2.1 Intention and Ethical Considerations

As conscious beings, we have the power to infuse intention and ethical considerations into our technological endeavors. By asking critical questions about the potential impact of technology on individuals, societies, and the environment, we can make informed decisions and actively shape the course of technological development.

2.2. Harnessing Technology for Human Growth

Technology, when harnessed consciously, can be a powerful tool for personal and collective growth. It offers opportunities for learning, creativity, and innovation. By using technology mindfully and with intention, we can leverage its potential to expand our consciousness, bridge divides, and address global challenges.

Embracing the Symbiotic Relationship

Recognizing the symbiotic relationship between human consciousness and technology allows us to navigate the digital age with wisdom and intention. It is not about rejecting or fearing technology but rather embracing it as a transformative force that can support our collective evolution. By cultivating awareness, discernment, and ethical considerations, we can shape technology to align with our values and support our well-being.

Conclusion

In this chapter, we explored the intersection of humanity and technology within the context of the 5D Mind. We recognized the influence of technology on our consciousness and the impact of our consciousness on the development and use of technology. By embracing this symbiotic relationship, we can harness technology consciously and ethically, ensuring its alignment with our highest values and aspirations. In the following chapters, we will delve deeper into practical strategies and insights for navigating the digital age, empowering us to thrive in harmony with technology while remaining connected to our core humanity.

Chapter 2
Cultivating a 5D Mindset

2.1
Awareness and Mindfulness: Techniques to enhance self-awareness and cultivate mindfulness in the digital age

Introduction

In Chapter 1, we explored the dimensions of the 5D Mind and their significance. In Chapter 2, we will delve into practical techniques and strategies for cultivating a 5D Mindset. This chapter focuses specifically on enhancing self-awareness and cultivating mindfulness in the digital age. By developing these skills, we can navigate the complexities of the modern world with clarity, presence, and intention.

Enhancing Self-Awareness

Self-awareness forms the foundation of a 5D Mindset. It involves developing a deep understanding of our thoughts, emotions, and actions, as well as our relationship with technology. Here are some techniques to enhance self- awareness:

1.1 Reflection and Self-Inquiry

Set aside dedicated time for reflection and self-inquiry. This can be done through journaling, meditation, or contemplative practices. Reflect on your experiences, emotions, and thoughts related to technology. Ask yourself questions such as: How does technology impact my well-being? What are my intentions and values in using technology? By engaging in self-inquiry, you gain insights into your relationship with technology and can make conscious choices that align with your authentic self.

1.2 Mindful Self-Observation

Practice mindful self-observation throughout the day. Observe your thoughts, emotions, and physical sensations as you engage with technology. Notice any patterns of reactivity, habitual behaviors, or emotional triggers that arise. By observing without judgment, you gain a greater understanding of your relationship with technology and can make conscious choices about your engagement. This practice also helps you develop a greater sense of presence and awareness in your everyday life.

Cultivating Mindfulness

Mindfulness is the practice of being fully present and engaged in the present moment. It allows us to develop a greater sense of clarity, focus, and calmness. Here are techniques to cultivate mindfulness in the digital age:

2.1 Mindful Technology Use

Bring mindfulness into your interactions with technology. Before engaging with digital devices or platforms, take a moment to set an intention for your use. Be fully present and engaged in the task at hand, minimizing distractions. Practice mindful breathing and body awareness to anchor yourself in the present moment. Notice any urges or impulses to mindlessly scroll or multitask, and consciously choose to redirect your attention to the present task.

2.2 Digital Detox and Mindful Breaks

Set aside regular periods for digital detoxes and mindful breaks. Disconnect from technology intentionally to recharge and reconnect with the present moment. Use this time for activities that nourish your well-being, such as spending time in nature, engaging in creative pursuits, or simply being fully present with loved ones. During mindful breaks, practice being fully engaged in the present moment without the need for external stimulation.

2.3 Setting Digital Boundaries

Establish clear boundaries around your digital engagement. Define specific times or spaces where technology use is limited or prohibited, such as during meals, before bedtime, or in certain areas of your home. Create a digital-free zone or time for increased focus, connection, and rejuvenation. By setting boundaries, you create space for intentional living and prevent technology from encroaching on every aspect of your life.

Conclusion

Chapter 2 has explored techniques for enhancing self-awareness and cultivating mindfulness in the digital age. By engaging in reflection, self-inquiry, mindful self-observation, and conscious technology use, we develop a deeper understanding of our relationship with technology and our own inner landscape. These practices allow us to navigate the digital world with greater clarity, intention, and presence, ensuring that technology becomes a tool for our growth and well-being rather than

2.2
Embracing Change and Uncertainty: Developing resilience and adaptability in the face of rapid technological advancements

Introduction

In Chapter 1, we explored the dimensions of the 5D Mind and their significance. In Chapter 2, we continue our journey by focusing on cultivating a 5D Mindset. This chapter dives into the importance of embracing change and uncertainty in the context of rapid technological advancements. By developing resilience and adaptability, we can navigate the ever-evolving digital landscape with confidence and grace.

Embracing Change

Change is an inherent part of the digital age. Technologies evolve at a rapid pace, shaping our lives in profound ways. To cultivate a 5D Mindset, it is essential to embrace change and recognize it as an opportunity for growth and transformation. Here are some strategies to embrace change:

1.1 .Cultivate a Growth Mindset

Adopt a growth mindset, which views challenges as opportunities for learning and growth. Embrace a belief that your abilities and intelligence can be developed through dedication and hard work. By seeing change as an avenue for personal and collective evolution, you become open to new possibilities and resilient in the face of challenges.

1.2 .Embrace Curiosity

Approach change with curiosity and a sense of wonder. Rather than resisting or fearing change, adopt an attitude of exploration and discovery. Curiosity allows you to see change as an opportunity to learn, innovate, and expand your horizons. Embrace the unknown with a sense of excitement and a willingness to explore new possibilities.

Developing Resilience

Resilience is the ability to adapt and bounce back in the face of challenges. In a world of rapid technological advancements, cultivating resilience is crucial for navigating uncertainties and setbacks. Here are techniques to develop resilience

2.1. Cultivate Self-Compassion

Practice self-compassion by treating yourself with kindness, understanding, and acceptance in times of change and uncertainty. Acknowledge that change can be challenging and that it is normal to experience a range of emotions. Be gentle with yourself and offer support and encouragement, just as you would to a close friend facing a similar situation.

2.2. Build a Supportive Network

Surround yourself with a supportive network of family, friends, mentors, and like-minded individuals. Seek out communities that share your interests and values, where you can find support, guidance, and inspiration during times of change. Collaborate with others, exchange ideas, and learn from their experiences to enhance your resilience.

Fostering Adaptability

Adaptability is the ability to adjust to new circumstances and navigate through uncertainty. It allows you to thrive in a rapidly changing world. Here are strategies to foster adaptability

3.1. Embrace Lifelong Learning

Adopt a mindset of lifelong learning. Stay curious and continuously seek knowledge and skills that align with the evolving digital landscape. Embrace new technologies, explore different fields, and cultivate a thirst for knowledge. By becoming a lifelong learner, you equip yourself with the adaptability needed to navigate change and thrive in a rapidly evolving world.

3.2. Develop Agility and Flexibility

Cultivate agility and flexibility in your thinking and actions. Be willing to let go of rigid beliefs, habits, and structures that no longer serve you in the face of change. Embrace a willingness to pivot, adjust, and explore new approaches and perspectives. Developing flexibility allows you to adapt to new technologies, challenges, and opportunities that arise.

Conclusion

Chapter 2 has focused on developing a 5D Mindset by embracing change and uncertainty. By cultivating resilience, embracing a growth mindset, and fostering adaptability, we can navigate the rapid technological advancements of the digital age.

2.3
Navigating Information Overload: Strategies for managing information overload and cultivating discernment in the digital era

Introduction

In Chapter 1, we explored the dimensions of the 5D Mind and their significance. In Chapter 2, we continue our exploration by focusing on cultivating a 5D Mindset. This chapter addresses the challenge of information overload in the digital era and provides strategies for managing it effectively. By developing discernment and adopting mindful practices, we can navigate the vast sea of information with clarity, purpose, and wisdom.

Understanding Information Overload

In the digital era, we are constantly bombarded with an overwhelming amount of information. This abundance of data can lead to information overload, making it challenging to filter through the noise and find valuable insights. Here are key strategies for managing information overload

1.1. Curate Your Information Sources

Take control of the information you consume by curating your sources. Evaluate the credibility, reliability, and relevance of the information providers. Prioritize quality over quantity, focusing on sources that align with your interests, values, and goals. Consider subscribing to newsletters, following thought leaders, and joining online communities that provide meaningful and reliable content.

1.2. Practice Selective Consumption

Be selective in what you consume and engage with. Recognize that you cannot consume all available information, and it is important to set boundaries. Prioritize the information that is most relevant to your goals and well-being. Avoid mindless scrolling or endless browsing and be intentional about the content you engage with.

Cultivating Discernment

Developing discernment is essential for navigating the vast amount of information available in the digital era. Discernment allows you to distinguish between reliable, valuable information and misinformation or irrelevant data. Here are strategies to cultivate discernment

2.1 Practice Critical Thinking

Engage in critical thinking when consuming information. Question the sources, assumptions, and biases present in the content. Evaluate the evidence provided and consider alternative perspectives. Develop a healthy skepticism and seek objective, verifiable information. By cultivating critical thinking skills, you become better equipped to discern reliable information from misinformation.

2.2. Fact-Checking and Verification

Verify information before accepting it as true. Fact-checking is crucial in an era of rampant misinformation. Cross-reference information from multiple reliable sources and consult reputable fact-checking organizations. Be cautious of spreading unverified information and contribute to a responsible and informed digital ecosystem.

Embracing Mindful Consumption

Mindful consumption involves being present and intentional in your engagement with digital information. It allows you to cultivate a balanced and meaningful relationship with the information you encounter. Here are strategies for embracing mindful consumption

3.1. Set Boundaries for Digital Consumption

Establish boundaries around your digital consumption. Determine specific times or durations for information consumption, and avoid excessive exposure to digital devices. Create designated technology-free zones or periods to foster presence, relaxation, and deeper connection with yourself and others.

3.2. Engage in Intentional Information Processing

Instead of mindlessly consuming information, engage in intentional processing. Pause and reflect on the information you encounter. Consider its relevance to your goals, values, and well-being. Reflect on how the information aligns with your authentic self and the impact it has on your thoughts, emotions, and actions.

Conclusion

Chapter 2 has explored strategies for managing information overload and cultivating discernment in the digital era. By curating your information sources, practicing selective consumption, developing critical thinking skills, fact-checking, and embracing mindful consumption, you can navigate the vast sea of information with clarity, purpose, and wisdom. These practices allow you to harness the power of information while maintaining a balanced and discerning approach.

Chapter 3
Harnessing the Power of Intuition

3.1
Awakening Intuitive Abilities: Techniques to tap into your innate intuition and develop trust in your inner guidance

Introduction

In Chapter 1, we explored the dimensions of the 5D Mind, and in Chapter 2, we focused on cultivating a 5D Mindset. In Chapter 3, we dive into the power of intuition and its role in navigating the digital age. Intuition serves as a compass, guiding us in making wise decisions and navigating complex situations. By awakening our intuitive abilities and developing trust in our inner guidance, we can access deeper wisdom and enhance our overall well- being.

Understanding Intuition

Intuition is a form of inner knowing that goes beyond logic and reasoning. It is a subtle, innate ability we all possess. Intuition helps us tap into deeper truths, insights, and guidance, guiding us in making choices aligned with our higher selves. Here are techniques to awaken your intuitive abilities

1.1.Cultivate Stillness and Silence

Create moments of stillness and silence in your daily life. Set aside time for meditation, contemplation, or simply being in nature. By quieting the mind and reducing external distractions, you create space for your intuition to emerge. Cultivating stillness allows you to listen to the whispers of your inner guidance.

1.2.Trust Your Gut Feelings

Pay attention to your gut feelings or "gut instincts." These intuitive sensations often arise as subtle nudges or feelings in the body. Practice noticing and trusting these feelings in various situations. Reflect on times when your intuition has guided you in the past and led to positive outcomes. By acknowledging and acting upon your gut feelings, you strengthen your intuitive connection.

Developing Trust in Your Inner Guidance

Trusting your inner guidance is crucial for harnessing the power of intuition. Here are techniques to develop trust in your inner guidance

2.1. Journaling and Reflection

Engage in journaling and reflection practices to explore and understand the guidance and insights that arise within you. Write down your intuitive experiences, dreams, and intuitive hunches. Reflect on these entries over time and observe patterns and themes. Journaling helps you develop a deeper understanding of your intuitive abilities and build trust in your inner guidance.

2.2.Act on Intuitive Prompts

Practice acting on your intuitive prompts, even when they may seem illogical or contrary to conventional wisdom. Start with small decisions and observe the outcomes. As you witness the positive effects of trusting your intuition, your trust in your inner guidance will grow. Gradually, you can apply your intuition to more significant decisions and areas of your life.

Cultivating Intuition in the Digital Age

In the digital age, it is important to cultivate intuition while navigating the vast amount of information and constant digital distractions. Here are strategies for cultivating intuition in the digital age

3.1.Digital Detox

Engage in regular digital detoxes to create space for intuition to thrive. Disconnect from digital devices and platforms intentionally. Allow yourself time away from the constant flow of information and external influences. Use this time for activities that foster presence, connection with nature, and self- reflection.

3.2.Mindful Technology Use

Practice mindful technology use by being present and engaged in your interactions with digital devices. Avoid mindless scrolling or excessive consumption of information. Set an intention for your technology use and notice how it aligns with your intuitive guidance. By being mindful, you can discern when to seek information and when to disconnect and tune into your inner wisdom.

Conclusion

Chapter 3 has explored the power of intuition and its role in navigating the digital age. By awakening your intuitive abilities through practices such as cultivating stillness, trusting your gut feelings, journaling, and acting on intuitive prompts, you can tap into your inner guidance. By developing trust in your intuition and practicing mindful technology use, you can harness the power of intuition to make wiser decisions and lead a more authentic and fulfilling life.

3.2
Embodying Emotional Intelligence: Understanding and managing emotions to make informed decisions in a digital world

Introduction

In Chapter 1, we explored the dimensions of the 5D Mind, and in Chapter 2, we focused on cultivating a 5D Mindset. In Chapter 3, we delve into the power of intuition. In addition to intuition, emotional intelligence plays a vital role in navigating the digital world. Embodying emotional intelligence allows us to understand and manage our emotions effectively, enabling us to make informed decisions and foster meaningful connections in the digital age.

Understanding Emotional Intelligence

Emotional intelligence refers to the ability to recognize, understand, and manage our own emotions, as well as to empathize with and relate to the emotions of others. It involves self-awareness, self-regulation, social awareness, and relationship management. Here are techniques to embody emotional intelligence

1.1. Cultivate Self-Awareness

Develop self-awareness by paying attention to your emotions and their underlying causes. Notice how different situations, interactions, and digital experiences impact your emotional state. Regular self-reflection and mindfulness practices can help you become more aware of your emotions in the digital world.

1.2. Practice Emotional Regulation

Learn to regulate your emotions by managing their intensity, duration, and expression. Recognize when you are experiencing intense emotions and take steps to calm yourself before making decisions or engaging in digital interactions. Deep breathing exercises, mindfulness meditation, and engaging in activities that bring you joy can help you regulate your emotions effectively.

Empathy and Social Awareness

Empathy is the ability to understand and share the feelings of others. In the digital world, fostering empathy and social awareness allows us to connect with others authentically. Here are techniques to cultivate empathy and social awareness

2.1. Practice Active Listening

Engage in active listening during digital interactions. Pay attention to not only the words being expressed but also the underlying emotions and intentions. Seek to understand the perspective of others and validate their emotions. Reflect back on what you have heard to ensure accurate comprehension and empathetic response.

2.2. Seek Diverse Perspectives

Expose yourself to diverse perspectives and experiences in the digital world. Follow individuals, groups, and platforms that provide diverse viewpoints. Engage in respectful and open-minded discussions that challenge your own assumptions and biases. By embracing diversity, you enhance your empathy and social awareness.

Making Informed Decisions in the Digital Age

Emotional intelligence plays a crucial role in making informed decisions amidst the vast amount of information and digital interactions. Here are strategies for making informed decisions in the digital age:

3.1. Pause and Reflect

Before making decisions in the digital realm, take a pause to reflect on your emotional state and how it may influence your judgment. Consider the long- term implications of your decisions and evaluate them from a holistic perspective. Taking the time to pause and reflect allows you to make choices aligned with your values and well-being.

3.2. Validate Information with Emotional Resonance

When evaluating information in the digital world, consider its emotional resonance with you. Notice if it evokes strong emotions or if it aligns with your intuitive sense of truth. Validate the information through multiple sources, fact-checking, and critical thinking. By considering the emotional aspect, you can make more informed and balanced decisions.

Conclusion

Chapter 3 has explored the importance of emotional intelligence in the digital age. By embodying emotional intelligence through self-awareness, emotional regulation, empathy, and social awareness, you can navigate the digital world with greater understanding and authenticity. By making informed decisions that consider both rationality and emotional resonance, you create a digital presence that is mindful, empathetic, and conducive to positive connections.

3.3
The Wisdom of the Heart: Exploring the heart's intelligence and its role in shaping our perceptions and actions

Introduction

In Chapter 1, we explored the dimensions of the 5D Mind, and in Chapter 2, we focused on cultivating a 5D Mindset. In Chapter 3, we continue our exploration by delving into the wisdom of the heart and its significance in navigating the digital age. The heart possesses its own intelligence, which goes beyond rationality and intuition. By understanding and accessing the wisdom of the heart, we can shape our perceptions and actions with greater authenticity and alignment.

The Heart's Intelligence

The heart is more than a physical organ; it is a center of intelligence that influences our thoughts, emotions, and actions. The heart's intelligence extends beyond logic and reasoning, offering insights that are deeply connected to our true selves and the world around us. Here are key aspects of the heart's intelligence

1.1. Intuitive Guidance

The heart serves as a powerful source of intuitive guidance. It communicates through feelings, emotions, and sensations. By tuning into the wisdom of the heart, we can access deeper insights and make decisions that are aligned with our highest good and the greater well-being of others.

1.2. Emotional Resonance

The heart has the ability to discern emotional resonance. It recognizes when something feels right or wrong, harmonious or discordant. By paying attention to the emotional responses that arise from the heart, we can gain clarity about our values, preferences, and the actions that best serve our growth and fulfillment.

Cultivating a Heart-Centered Approach

Cultivating a heart-centered approach allows us to align our perceptions and actions with the wisdom of the heart. Here are techniques for cultivating a heart-centered approach

2.1. Heart-Centered Practices

Engage in heart-centered practices such as heart-focused meditation, heart coherence exercises, or heart-opening rituals. These practices help us connect with the energy and intelligence of the heart, fostering a sense of compassion, love, and interconnectedness.

2.2. Cultivating Compassion

Practice cultivating compassion towards yourself and others. The heart's intelligence is intimately linked to empathy and compassion. By consciously cultivating compassion, we open ourselves to a deeper understanding of the human experience and act from a place of kindness, empathy, and love.

Integrating the Heart's Wisdom in the Digital Age

In the digital age, it is crucial to integrate the wisdom of the heart into our digital interactions and decision-making. Here are strategies for integrating the heart's wisdom in the digital age.

3.1. Mindful Digital Engagement

Approach digital engagement with mindfulness and presence. Before posting or responding to online content, take a moment to check in with your heart. Notice how it feels and if the content aligns with your values and intentions. Let the wisdom of the heart guide your interactions, promoting empathy, respect, and constructive dialogue.

3.2. Authentic Self-Expression

Allow the wisdom of the heart to shape your authentic self-expression in the digital realm. Share your thoughts, ideas, and experiences from a place of genuine authenticity. Speak from the heart, expressing your truth with clarity, compassion, and integrity. By embodying the wisdom of the heart, you contribute to a more heart-centered digital space.

Conclusion

Chapter 3 has explored the wisdom of the heart and its role in shaping our perceptions and actions. By tapping into the heart's intelligence through intuitive guidance and emotional resonance, we can navigate the digital age with greater authenticity and alignment. By cultivating a heart-centered approach and integrating the wisdom of the heart in our digital interactions, we contribute to a more compassionate, connected, and meaningful digital world.

Chapter 4
Creating Connection in a Digital World

4.1
Authentic Communication: Nurturing genuine connections and fostering meaningful relationships in the digital realm

Introduction

In Chapter 1, we explored the dimensions of the 5D Mind, in Chapter 2, we focused on cultivating a 5D Mindset, and in Chapter 3, we delved into the power of intuition and the wisdom of the heart. In Chapter 4, we shift our focus to creating connections in the digital world. Authentic communication lies at the heart of meaningful relationships, and nurturing genuine connections is essential in the digital realm. By embracing authentic communication, we can foster deep connections and enrich our digital experiences.

The Importance of Authentic Communication

Authentic communication is rooted in honesty, vulnerability, and genuine expression. In the digital world, where communication often takes place through screens and devices, it is essential to prioritize authentic communication to build meaningful connections. Here are key aspects of authentic communication.

1.1. Honesty and Transparency

Authentic communication requires honesty and transparency in expressing oneself. It involves sharing thoughts, emotions, and experiences genuinely, without pretense or facade. By being truthful and transparent in our digital interactions, we foster trust and authenticity.

1.2. Active Listening and Empathy

Authentic communication goes beyond self-expression; it also involves active listening and empathetic understanding. By truly listening to others and seeking to understand their perspectives and emotions, we create a space for genuine connection and mutual growth.

Cultivating Authentic Communication

Cultivating authentic communication skills is a continuous practice that allows us to deepen our connections in the digital world. Here are techniques for cultivating authentic communication

2.1. Cultivate Self-Awareness

Develop self-awareness around your communication patterns, including your tone, language, and intention behind your words. Reflect on how your communication impacts others and how it aligns with your values. By cultivating self-awareness, you can make conscious choices in your digital interactions.

2.2. Practice Mindful Communication

Engage in mindful communication by being fully present during conversations and digital exchanges. Avoid distractions and give your undivided attention to the person or group you are engaging with. Respond thoughtfully and respectfully, considering the impact of your words on others.

Fostering Meaningful Connections in the Digital Realm

In the digital realm, it is important to foster meaningful connections beyond surface-level interactions. Here are strategies for fostering meaningful connections in the digital world

3.1. Authentic Storytelling

Share personal stories and experiences authentically. By opening up and sharing vulnerable aspects of your life, you invite others to connect with you on a deeper level. Authentic storytelling creates a sense of empathy and shared experiences, strengthening the bonds of connection.

3. 2. Engage in Meaningful Dialogue

Participate in meaningful dialogue by engaging in conversations that go beyond small talk and surface-level topics. Encourage open and honest discussions about ideas, values, and experiences. Create spaces where diverse perspectives are respected and where individuals can express themselves authentically.

Nurturing Digital Relationships

Nurturing digital relationships requires effort and intentionality. Here are practices for nurturing digital relationships

4.1. Regular Check-ins

Make an effort to regularly check in with your digital connections. Reach out, ask how they are doing, and show genuine interest in their lives. By nurturing these relationships, you create a sense of care and belonging in the digital realm.

4.2. Cultivate Empathy and Compassion

Approach your digital interactions with empathy and compassion. Seek to understand the emotions and experiences of others, and respond with kindness and understanding. By cultivating empathy and compassion, you create a supportive and nurturing digital environment.

Conclusion

Chapter 4 has emphasized the importance of authentic communication in nurturing genuine connections and fostering meaningful relationships in the digital world. By practicing honesty, transparency, active listening, and empathy, we can create spaces for authentic communication to thrive. By engaging in mindful communication, fostering meaningful connections, and nurturing digital relationships, we contribute to a digital realm that is characterized by authenticity, empathy, and deep connection.

4.2
Empathy and Compassion: Cultivating empathy and compassion for ourselves and others amidst technological interactions

Introduction

In Chapter 1, we explored the dimensions of the 5D Mind, in Chapter 2, we focused on cultivating a 5D Mindset, in Chapter 3, we delved into the power of intuition and the wisdom of the heart, and now, in Chapter 4, we shift our focus to creating connections in the digital world. Empathy and compassion play a vital role in fostering meaningful relationships and nurturing a sense of belonging, both online and offline. In this chapter, we will explore the importance of cultivating empathy and compassion in the digital realm.

Understanding Empathy and Compassion

Empathy is the ability to understand and share the feelings of others, while compassion is the desire to alleviate their suffering. These qualities are essential in creating a sense of connection and fostering a supportive digital environment. Here are key aspects of empathy and compassion.

1.1. Emotional Resonance

Empathy begins with recognizing and resonating with the emotions of others. It involves putting ourselves in their shoes and genuinely understanding their experiences and perspectives. Emotional resonance allows us to connect on a deeper level and respond with compassion.

1.2. Alleviating Suffering

Compassion moves us to take action and alleviate the suffering of others. In the digital realm, this can involve offering support, providing resources, or simply offering a listening ear. Compassion helps create a sense of community and support in the face of challenges.

Cultivating Empathy and Compassion

Cultivating empathy and compassion is a practice that can be nurtured and developed. Here are techniques for cultivating empathy and compassion in the digital realm.

2.1. Practice Active Listening

Engage in active listening during digital interactions. Pay attention not only to the words being expressed but also to the emotions underlying them. Validate the feelings of others and seek to understand their experiences without judgment. Active listening fosters empathy and creates a safe space for open communication.

2.2. Cultivate Self-Compassion

Extend compassion to yourself by recognizing your own emotions, needs, and struggles. Treat yourself with kindness and understanding, especially in the face of challenges or digital negativity. By cultivating self-compassion, you can model empathy and compassion for others.

Promoting Empathy and Compassion in the Digital Realm

In the digital realm, empathy and compassion are crucial in promoting a sense of connection and well-being. Here are strategies for promoting empathy and compassion in the digital world

3.1. Cultivate Digital Empathy

Recognize that behind every online profile and interaction, there is a human being with emotions and experiences. Practice empathy by considering the feelings and perspectives of others before responding or engaging in online discussions. Foster a culture of empathy that encourages understanding and respectful dialogue.

3.2. Spread Positivity and Support

Make a conscious effort to spread positivity and support in the digital world. Offer words of encouragement, acknowledge the achievements of others, and provide emotional support when needed. Small acts of kindness can make a significant impact on someone's well-being and foster a compassionate digital environment.

Mindful Technology Use

Practice mindful technology use to foster empathy and compassion in the digital realm. Set boundaries and allocate dedicated time for offline connections and self-care. By nurturing your own well-being, you can show up with greater empathy and compassion in your online interactions.

Conclusion

Chapter 4 has emphasized the importance of cultivating empathy and compassion in the digital realm. By practicing active listening, cultivating self-compassion, and promoting empathy and compassion in our digital interactions, we contribute to a more supportive and compassionate digital world. By nurturing empathy and compassion for ourselves and others, we foster meaningful connections and create a sense of belonging amidst technological interactions.

4.3
Balancing Virtual and Physical Presence: Finding harmony between online engagement and the importance of face-to-face connections

Introduction

In Chapter 1, we explored the dimensions of the 5D Mind, in Chapter 2, we focused on cultivating a 5D Mindset, in Chapter 3, we delved into the power of intuition and the wisdom of the heart, and in Chapter 4, we discussed the significance of authentic communication, empathy, and compassion in fostering meaningful connections in the digital realm. In this section, we will explore the importance of finding a balance between virtual and physical presence, recognizing the value of both online engagement and face-to-face connections.

The Role of Online Engagement

Online engagement has revolutionized the way we connect with others, expanding our reach and opportunities for communication. Here are key aspects of online engagement

1.1. Global Reach

Through the digital world, we can connect with individuals from all around the globe, transcending geographical boundaries and cultural barriers. Online engagement allows us to broaden our perspectives and engage with diverse communities and ideas.

1.2. Convenience and Accessibility

The digital realm offers convenience and accessibility, enabling us to connect with others at any time and from anywhere. It provides a platform for instant communication, information sharing, and collaboration.

The Importance of Face-to-Face Connections

While online engagement offers numerous benefits, it is equally crucial to recognize the value of face-to-face connections. Here are key aspects of face- to-face connections

2.1. Depth and Authenticity

Face-to-face interactions provide a deeper level of connection and authenticity. Non-verbal cues, such as body language and facial expressions, contribute to a richer understanding of others and enhance communication.

2.2. Emotional Connection

Being physically present with others allows for a more profound emotional connection. Shared experiences, gestures, and the energy exchanged in person contribute to a sense of belonging and intimacy.

Finding Balance and Harmony

To fully embrace the digital world while nourishing our need for face-to-face connections, it is important to find balance and harmony. Here are strategies for finding balance.

3.1. Mindful Technology Use

Practice mindful technology use by setting boundaries and establishing designated times for online engagement. Create tech-free zones or periods to prioritize face-to-face interactions and fully immerse yourself in the present moment.

3.2. Prioritizing Offline Connections

Recognize the importance of offline connections and make them a priority. Dedicate time to spend with loved ones, engage in meaningful conversations, and participate in activities that foster real-world connections.

3.3. Blending Virtual and Physical Worlds

Integrate the virtual and physical realms by organizing gatherings, events, or meet-ups with online communities or friends. This allows for the transition from digital interactions to meaningful face-to-face connections.

Cultivating Presence in Both Realms

Whether in the digital or physical realm, cultivating presence is essential. Here are practices to cultivate presence in both realms.

4.1. Mindful Digital Engagement

Engage in mindful digital engagement by being fully present during online interactions. Focus on the conversation at hand, actively listen, and respond thoughtfully. Avoid multitasking or becoming overwhelmed by excessive online stimuli.

4.2. Active Participation in Real-World Interactions

When engaging in face-to-face connections, practice active participation by being fully present and engaged. Give your undivided attention, listen attentively, and foster meaningful exchanges. Embrace the moment and the connections that arise from it.

Conclusion

Chapter 4 has highlighted the importance of finding balance and harmony between virtual and physical presence in the digital world. By recognizing the value of both online engagement and face-to-face connections, we can foster meaningful connections, broaden our perspectives, and create a sense of belonging. By practicing mindful technology use, prioritizing offline connections, and cultivating presence in both realms, we create a harmonious balance that enriches our overall human experience.

Chapter 5
Expanding Consciousness
Through Technology

5.1
Conscious Media Consumption: Choosing mindfully and engaging with media that uplifts and expands our consciousness

Introduction

In Chapter 1, we explored the dimensions of the 5D Mind, in Chapter 2, we focused on cultivating a 5D Mindset, in Chapter 3, we delved into the power of intuition and the wisdom of the heart, in Chapter 4, we discussed creating connections in a digital world, and now, in Chapter 5, we will explore how technology can be a tool for expanding consciousness. Specifically, we will delve into conscious media consumption and the importance of mindfully choosing and engaging with media that uplifts and expands our consciousness.

The Influence of Media

Media plays a significant role in shaping our thoughts, beliefs, and perceptions. In the digital age, we have access to a vast array of media content, ranging from news articles and social media posts to videos, podcasts, and films. Here are key aspects of media influence

1.1. Information and Entertainment

Media provides us with information, entertainment, and opportunities for connection. However, not all media content is created equal, and it is crucial to be discerning in our choices to ensure we engage with content that supports our growth and well-being.

1.2. Impact on Consciousness

The media we consume has a direct impact on our consciousness. It can shape our worldview, influence our emotions, and affect our overall well-being. By consciously selecting media that expands our consciousness, we can elevate our thoughts, broaden our perspectives, and enhance our understanding of the world.

Conscious Media Consumption

Conscious media consumption involves mindfully choosing and engaging with media content that aligns with our values, uplifts our consciousness, and supports our personal growth. Here are strategies for conscious media consumption.

2.1. Clarify Your Intentions

Before engaging with media, clarify your intentions. Are you seeking information, inspiration, or entertainment? By being clear about your intentions, you can make conscious choices that align with your desired outcome.

2.2. Seek Diverse Perspectives

Expose yourself to a variety of perspectives and voices. Engage with content that challenges your beliefs and broadens your understanding of different cultures, ideas, and experiences. Seek out diverse voices and platforms that promote inclusivity and equality.

2.3. Evaluate Content

Develop critical thinking skills to evaluate the content you consume. Consider the credibility of the source, fact-check information before accepting it as truth, and be mindful of biases or sensationalism. Choose media that presents balanced views and encourages thoughtful analysis.

Uplifting and Expanding Consciousness

Engaging with media that uplifts and expands our consciousness can have profound effects on our personal growth and well-being. Here are ways to incorporate uplifting media into your life

3.1. Inspiring and Educational Content

Choose media that inspires and educates you. Seek out documentaries, TED Talks, podcasts, and books that explore topics such as personal development, spirituality, mindfulness, and positive social change. These resources can expand your knowledge and inspire transformative insights.

3.2. Creative Expression

Engage with creative forms of media, such as art, music, and literature, that evoke emotions and stimulate your imagination. These mediums can connect you with deeper aspects of yourself and enhance your capacity for empathy and self-expression.

Creating Conscious Media

Beyond being consumers of media, consider becoming creators of conscious media. Use technology as a platform to share your unique voice, insights, and stories. By contributing to the creation of conscious media, you can inspire and uplift others, fostering positive change in the digital landscape.

Conclusion

Chapter 5 has highlighted the significance of conscious media consumption in expanding consciousness through technology. By mindfully choosing and engaging with media that uplifts, inspires, and expands our perspectives, we can transform our digital experiences into powerful tools for personal growth, understanding, and positive change. By incorporating conscious media consumption into our lives, we contribute to a collective expansion of consciousness in the digital age.

5.2
Virtual Reality and Augmented Reality: Exploring the potential of immersive technologies to expand our perception and understanding

Introduction

In Chapter 1, we explored the dimensions of the 5D Mind, in Chapter 2, we focused on cultivating a 5D Mindset, in Chapter 3, we delved into the power of intuition and the wisdom of the heart, in Chapter 4, we discussed creating connections in a digital world, and in the previous section, Chapter 5.1, we explored the importance of conscious media consumption. Now, in Chapter 5.2, we will dive into the realm of virtual reality (VR) and augmented reality (AR) and explore how these immersive technologies have the potential to expand our perception and understanding.

The Rise of Immersive Technologies

Immersive technologies such as virtual reality (VR) and augmented reality (AR) have rapidly evolved in recent years, offering new ways to engage with digital content. These technologies create interactive, simulated environments or enhance the real-world environment with virtual elements. Here are key aspects of immersive technologies:

1.1. Virtual Reality (VR)

VR creates a completely immersive digital environment that simulates reality, transporting users to computer-generated worlds through specialized headsets and controllers. It offers a sense of presence and allows users to interact with the virtual environment.

1.2. Augmented Reality (AR)

AR overlays virtual elements onto the real-world environment, enhancing our perception and interaction with the physical world. AR technology utilizes smartphones, tablets, or specialized glasses to superimpose virtual objects, information, or experiences onto our immediate surroundings.

Expanding Perception and Understanding

VR and AR have the potential to expand our perception and understanding in various ways. Here are some areas where these technologies can make a significant impact

2.1. Immersive Learning Experiences

VR and AR provide immersive learning experiences that go beyond traditional educational methods. They can transport learners to different historical periods, simulate scientific experiments, or offer interactive language and cultural immersion. These technologies make learning engaging, experiential, and memorable.

2.2. Empathy and Perspective Taking

VR and AR have the power to foster empathy and understanding by allowing users to step into the shoes of others. They can simulate experiences that provide insights into different perspectives, cultures, or challenging life situations, fostering empathy and promoting social awareness.

2.3. Simulation and Training

Immersive technologies enable realistic simulations and training scenarios in various fields. From medical training and disaster preparedness to professional skills development, VR and AR provide a safe and controlled environment for practice and skill enhancement.

Ethical Considerations

As with any technological advancement, there are ethical considerations to be mindful of when utilizing immersive technologies

3.1. Content Curation

Careful curation of VR and AR content is essential to ensure that it aligns with ethical standards and promotes positive and constructive experiences. Content creators and users should be mindful of potential negative impacts and strive for responsible content creation and consumption.

3.2. User Well-being

Extended use of immersive technologies may have physical and psychological implications. It is important to prioritize user well-being by promoting breaks, proper ergonomics, and considering potential motion sickness or psychological discomfort.

Harnessing the Potential

To harness the potential of immersive technologies for expanding consciousness, it is crucial to approach their usage mindfully and responsibly. Here are some strategies for utilizing VR and AR in a conscious manner.

4.1. Intentional Engagement

Set clear intentions before using VR or AR experiences. Reflect on the purpose of the experience and how it can contribute to your personal growth, understanding, or well-being. Approach the technology with a curious and open mindset.

4.2. Critical Analysis

Apply critical thinking skills when engaging with immersive content. Consider the credibility and accuracy of the information presented. Question assumptions, biases, or potential distortions within the virtual or augmented environment.

4.3. Integration with Other Practices

Combine the use of immersive technologies with other practices that support expansion of consciousness, such as mindfulness, meditation, reflection, and discussions with others. This integration can enhance the transformative potential of the experiences.

Conclusion

Chapter 5.2 has explored the potential of immersive technologies, specifically virtual reality (VR) and augmented reality (AR), to expand our perception and understanding. By embracing these technologies mindfully, setting clear intentions, and critically analyzing the content, we can tap into their transformative power to enhance learning, empathy, and perspective taking. As we navigate the intersection of technology and consciousness, we have the opportunity to explore new dimensions of reality and expand our understanding of ourselves and the world around us.

5.3
Artificial Intelligence and Human Collaboration: Embracing the partnership between humans and AI for collective growth and progress

Introduction

In Chapter 1, we explored the dimensions of the 5D Mind, in Chapter 2, we focused on cultivating a 5D Mindset, in Chapter 3, we delved into the power of intuition and the wisdom of the heart, in Chapter 4, we discussed creating connections in a digital world, and in the previous sections of Chapter 5, we explored conscious media consumption and the potential of immersive technologies. Now, in Chapter 5.3, we will explore the partnership between humans and artificial intelligence (AI) and how it can contribute to expanding consciousness for collective growth and progress.

The Rise of Artificial Intelligence (AI)

Artificial intelligence refers to computer systems or machines that can perform tasks that typically require human intelligence. AI has advanced significantly in recent years, and its integration into various aspects of our lives has become increasingly prevalent. Here are key aspects of AI.

1.1. Machine Learning and Neural Networks

AI systems employ machine learning algorithms and neural networks to analyze vast amounts of data, identify patterns, and make informed decisions. Through continuous learning, AI systems can improve their performance over time.

1.2. Applications in Various Fields

AI finds applications in various fields, including healthcare, finance, transportation, education, and entertainment. It assists in data analysis, automation, prediction, and decision-making processes, augmenting human capabilities.

Human-AI Partnership for Collective Growth

Rather than viewing AI as a replacement for humans, we can embrace it as a tool for collaboration and partnership. The integration of AI into our lives presents opportunities for collective growth and progress. Here are key aspects of the human-AI partnership.

2.1. Complementing Human Skills

AI can complement human skills and abilities, augmenting our capabilities in various domains. It can assist in complex data analysis, provide personalized recommendations, and automate repetitive tasks, freeing up human potential for higher-level thinking and creativity.

2.2. Enhanced Problem-Solving

By harnessing the power of AI, we can address complex challenges and solve problems more effectively. AI systems can process vast amounts of data and identify patterns that may be beyond human capacity, leading to innovative solutions and insights.

2.3. Ethical Considerations

As we embrace the partnership between humans and AI, it is crucial to consider ethical implications. Transparency, accountability, and ensuring that AI systems align with human values and ethical frameworks are essential for responsible AI development and usage.

Collaboration and Co-Creation

To leverage the potential of AI for expanding consciousness, we can adopt a collaborative and co-creative approach. Here are strategies for embracing the partnership between humans and AI.

3.1. Learning and Adaptation

Continuously learn about AI advancements, understand its capabilities and limitations, and adapt to its integration into various aspects of our lives. Cultivate a growth mindset and embrace lifelong learning to stay informed and engaged.

3.2. Ethical Frameworks

Promote the development and adoption of ethical frameworks for AI. Engage in discussions and contribute to the establishment of guidelines that prioritize human well-being, inclusivity, fairness, and transparency.

3.3. Human-Centric Design

Advocate for human-centric AI design. Ensure that AI systems are designed to enhance human experiences, empower individuals, and promote collective well-being. Consider the potential social impact and work towards creating AI technologies that foster positive change.

Conclusion

Chapter 5.3 has highlighted the partnership between humans and artificial intelligence (AI) as a means of expanding consciousness for collective growth and progress. By embracing the potential of AI, complementing human skills, and adopting ethical frameworks, we can harness the power of AI to address complex challenges, enhance problem-solving, and co-create a future that aligns with our values and aspirations. As we navigate the evolving landscape of technology, the collaboration between humans and AI opens up new horizons for expanding our consciousness and shaping a better world.

Elevating Corporate Consciousness for Success in the Digital Age

Introduction

Welcome to the world of the 5D MIND, where ancient wisdom meets modern innovation, and corporate leaders embark on a transformative journey towards success in the dynamic digital age. This book is a guide for corporates who seek to harness the full potential of their organizations by embracing a new paradigm of thinking and leading in the fifth dimension.

Conclusion

Embrace the 5D MIND to unlock the full potential of your corporate, uplift the collective consciousness, and navigate the complexities of the digital age with grace and wisdom. May this journey empower you to lead your organization towards sustainable success and create a positive impact on the world. Remember, the 5D MIND is not just a destination, but an ongoing evolution of corporate consciousness.

Chapter 1
The Digital Age and the Need for 5D Thinking

Introduction:

The digital age has ushered in a period of unprecedented change and disruption across industries. Technology advancements, rapid globalization, and evolving customer expectations have transformed the business landscape. In this chapter, we will explore the profound impact of the digital age on businesses and the compelling need for adopting a 5D MIND approach to thrive in this new era. We will delve into why linear thinking is no longer sufficient and how 5D thinking can unlock creativity, innovation, and adaptability.

1.1 The Era of Digital Transformation:

The digital age has brought about a seismic shift in the way businesses operate. Organizations that fail to adapt risk being left behind, as traditional business models struggle to keep up with the pace of technological advancements. Digital transformation is no longer a buzzword but a necessity for survival. Companies must embrace new technologies, harness the power of data and analytics, and leverage digital channels to remain competitive and relevant.

1.2 The Limitations of Linear Thinking:

Linear thinking, characterized by a step-by-step, cause-and-effect approach, has long been the foundation of traditional business practices. However, in the digital age, linear thinking alone is insufficient. The complexities and interconnectedness of today's business ecosystem require a more holistic and dynamic approach.

Linear thinking often leads to narrow-mindedness and tunnel vision, inhibiting organizations from exploring unconventional ideas or embracing change. It restricts creativity, innovation, and adaptability, which are essential qualities for success in the digital era. To thrive, businesses must transition to a multidimensional mindset.

1.3 Introducing 5D Thinking:

5D thinking represents a paradigm shift, expanding beyond the constraints of linear thought processes. It encompasses a multidimensional approach that considers various dimensions of business and leadership. By adopting 5D thinking, organizations can tap into their full potential, adapt to change, and seize new opportunities in the digital age.

1.4 The Five Dimensions of 5D Thinking:

1. **Dimension of Self-Awareness:** The first dimension of 5D thinking involves cultivating self-awareness among leaders and individuals within the organization. Self-awareness enhances emotional intelligence, promotes authentic leadership, and encourages introspection. By understanding their strengths, weaknesses, values, and biases, leaders can make informed decisions, build meaningful relationships, and inspire others.

2. **Dimension of Innovation:** The dimension of innovation embraces a culture of creativity, experimentation, and openness to new ideas. It encourages organizations to embrace a growth mindset and nurture an environment where innovation can flourish. By fostering a culture that encourages calculated risk-taking, problem- solving, and continuous learning, businesses can stay ahead of the curve and drive sustainable growth.

3. **Dimension of Collaboration:** Collaboration is crucial in the digital age, as interconnectedness and teamwork become increasingly vital. Breaking down silos and fostering collaboration across departments, teams, and even external stakeholders enables organizations to leverage diverse perspectives, collective intelligence, and shared resources. Collaboration empowers individuals to work together towards common goals, enhancing productivity and decision-making.

4. **Dimension of Sustainability:** In the digital age, businesses must embrace sustainability in all its dimensions — environmental, social, and economic. Sustainability entails responsible practices that minimize environmental impact, prioritize social well-being, and drive long-term economic viability. Organizations that integrate sustainability into

their core strategies not only mitigate risks but also gain a competitive edge, attract conscious customers, and contribute positively to society.

5. **Dimension of Future Vision:** The dimension of future vision involves developing foresight and strategic planning to anticipate industry trends and market shifts. By envisioning future scenarios, organizations can proactively shape their strategies, products, and services to meet evolving customer needs. Future-focused thinking allows businesses to adapt and innovate ahead of the curve, transforming challenges into opportunities.

Conclusion:

The digital age demands a departure from linear thinking and the adoption of a multidimensional mindset. The 5D MIND framework offers a holistic approach that embraces self-awareness, innovation, collaboration, sustainability, and future vision. By transcending linear thought processes, organizations can unlock their creative potential, foster innovation, and adapt to the rapidly changing business landscape. In the subsequent chapters, we will delve deeper into each dimension of the 5D MIND, providing practical insights and strategies for implementation.

Chapter 2
The Five Dimensions of 5D MIND

In Chapter 1, we introduced the concept of 5D thinking and its relevance in the digital age. Now, let's delve deeper into each dimension of the 5D MIND framework. Each dimension represents a crucial aspect of corporate consciousness that, when integrated, empowers organizations to thrive in the dynamic and ever-evolving business landscape.

2.1 Dimension of Self-Awareness:

The foundation of the 5D MIND framework lies in self-awareness. This dimension involves cultivating mindfulness and emotional intelligence among corporate leaders and employees. Self-awareness allows individuals to understand their emotions, motivations, strengths, and limitations. By developing a deep sense of self-awareness, leaders can make conscious decisions, manage their emotions effectively, and lead with authenticity.

Benefits of Self-Awareness:

- **Improved decision-making:** Self-aware leaders are better equipped to assess situations objectively and make informed choices.

- **Authentic leadership:** Leaders who understand themselves can lead from a place of authenticity, earning trust and respect from their teams.

- **Conflict resolution:** Self-awareness fosters empathy, which is crucial in resolving conflicts and building strong relationships within the organization.

2.2 Dimension of Innovation:

Innovation is the lifeblood of successful businesses in the digital age. The dimension of innovation encourages organizations to embrace creativity and experimentation, creating a culture where new ideas are nurtured and celebrated. It involves challenging the status quo, promoting a growth mindset, and being open to taking calculated risks.

Benefits of Innovation:

- **Competitive advantage:** Innovative companies stand out in crowded markets, gaining a competitive edge.

- **Agility and adaptability:** Innovative organizations are better equipped to adapt to changing circumstances and disruptions.

- **Customer-centricity:** Innovation enables companies to create products and services that meet evolving customer needs.

2.3 Dimension of Collaboration:

The dimension of collaboration emphasizes the power of teamwork and interconnectedness within an organization. It involves breaking down silos and fostering a culture of collaboration, where diverse perspectives are valued, and collective intelligence is harnessed to solve problems and drive results.

Benefits of Collaboration:

- **Enhanced creativity:** Collaboration sparks creativity through the exchange of ideas and perspectives from different individuals.

- **Improved problem-solving:** Diverse teams can tackle complex problems with a broader range of solutions.

- **Increased employee engagement:** A collaborative environment empowers employees, boosting their sense of ownership and motivation.

2.4 Dimension of Sustainability:

Sustainability is no longer a mere buzzword but a vital consideration for businesses in the digital age. The dimension of sustainability encompasses responsible practices that prioritize environmental stewardship, social responsibility, and long-term economic viability.

Benefits of Sustainability:

- **Reputation and brand value:** Sustainability initiatives enhance a company's reputation, attracting conscious customers and stakeholders.

- **Risk mitigation:** Sustainable practices reduce environmental and social risks, leading to a more resilient organization.

- **Employee attraction and retention:** A commitment to sustainability attracts purpose-driven employees, enhancing talent retention.

2.5 Dimension of Future Vision:

The final dimension of 5D MIND is future vision, which involves strategic foresight and planning. It requires organizations to anticipate industry trends, emerging technologies, and changing customer preferences to stay ahead of the curve.

Benefits of Future Vision:

- **Proactive strategy:** Future-focused organizations can proactively shape their strategies, rather than being reactive to market changes.

- **Innovation direction:** A clear future vision guides innovation efforts toward meeting upcoming challenges and opportunities.

- **Investor confidence:** A strong future vision instills confidence in investors and stakeholders, driving support and investment.

Conclusion:

The 5D MIND framework comprises five interconnected dimensions: self- awareness, innovation, collaboration, sustainability, and future vision. Each dimension brings unique benefits to an organization, fostering a conscious and agile corporate culture that thrives in the digital age. In the following chapters, we will explore practical strategies for implementing and integrating these dimensions into various aspects of corporate life, propelling your organization towards sustainable success and positive impact.

Chapter 3
Implementing the 5D MIND Framework

In Chapter 2, we explored the five dimensions of the 5D MIND framework. Now, let's focus on how to effectively integrate these dimensions into different aspects of corporate life. By implementing the 5D MIND framework in leadership development, talent management, employee engagement, and organizational culture, businesses can create a conscious, innovative, and adaptive ecosystem that thrives in the digital age.

3.1 Leadership Development:

Leadership plays a pivotal role in shaping the culture and direction of an organization. Implementing the 5D MIND framework in leadership development involves nurturing leaders with a deep understanding of themselves, their teams, and their impact on the organization. Here are practical strategies to achieve this:

a) Self-awareness workshops: Conduct workshops and training sessions to promote self-awareness among leaders. Encourage introspection, emotional intelligence development, and mindfulness practices to enhance their ability to lead with authenticity.

b) Innovation leadership programs: Foster a culture of innovation by providing leaders with training and resources to encourage creativity, experimentation, and risk-taking.

c) Collaborative leadership initiatives: Emphasize the importance of collaboration and teamwork in leadership roles. Encourage leaders to build strong relationships and embrace diverse perspectives to enhance decision- making and problem-solving.

d) Sustainable leadership practices: Integrate sustainability principles into leadership development programs, emphasizing responsible decision- making, and long-term thinking.

e) Visionary leadership training: Develop future-oriented leadership capabilities by providing leaders with tools to anticipate industry trends, identify emerging opportunities, and create a compelling vision for the organization.

3.2 Talent Management:

Attracting, developing, and retaining top talent is critical for organizational success. Integrating the 5D MIND framework into talent management practices involves aligning recruitment, training, and career growth initiatives with the dimensions of 5D thinking.

a) Recruitment for cultural fit: During the hiring process, assess candidates not only for their skills but also for their alignment with the organization's values and commitment to sustainability and collaboration.

b) Innovation-focused training: Offer ongoing training programs that foster innovation and creativity, ensuring employees are equipped with the skills and mindset to drive the organization forward.

c) Cross-functional exposure: Encourage cross-functional collaboration and rotation, allowing employees to gain diverse experiences and develop a broader perspective.

d) Sustainability initiatives: Involve employees in sustainability efforts, empowering them to contribute to the organization's sustainable practices and social impact.

e) Future-focused career paths: Create development paths that align with the organization's future vision, empowering employees to see their growth opportunities within the context of the company's long-term goals.

3.3 Employee Engagement:

Engaged employees are more productive, innovative, and committed to the organization's success. Implementing the 5D MIND framework into employee engagement strategies can foster a positive and purpose-driven work environment.

a) Empowerment and autonomy: Encourage employee autonomy, enabling them to take ownership of their work and contribute to decision-making processes.

b) Recognition and rewards: Recognize and reward employees who demonstrate self-awareness, innovative thinking, collaboration, and sustainability efforts.

c) Collaborative projects: Promote cross-functional projects that allow employees to work together and learn from one another's expertise.

d) Sustainability initiatives: Involve employees in sustainability programs and social impact activities, fostering a sense of purpose and contribution.

e) Future vision alignment: Communicate the organization's future vision to employees, ensuring they understand their roles in achieving long-term objectives.

3.4 Organizational Culture:

The organizational culture serves as the foundation for 5D MIND implementation. To create a culture that embraces the 5D MIND framework, leaders must be role models and actively encourage these dimensions throughout the organization.

a) Values-driven culture: Align the organizational values with the principles of 5D MIND, making them the core of decision-making and operations.

b) Continuous learning: Promote a culture of continuous learning and development, encouraging employees to grow and adapt to new challenges and opportunities.

c) Innovation hubs: Establish innovation hubs or designated spaces where employees can freely brainstorm and experiment with new ideas.

d) Collaboration platforms: Utilize digital tools and platforms that facilitate collaboration and knowledge sharing among employees.

e) Sustainability practices: Implement sustainability initiatives at all levels of the organization, from resource management to waste reduction.

Conclusion:

Implementing the 5D MIND framework requires a commitment to transformational change within the organization. By integrating these dimensions into leadership development, talent management, employee engagement, and organizational culture, businesses can create a conscious and adaptive ecosystem that fosters creativity, innovation, and long-term success in the digital age. Embrace the 5D MIND framework and propel your organization towards a brighter and more sustainable future.

Chapter 4
Overcoming Challenges in
Embracing 5D Thinking

As with any significant organizational transformation, embracing the 5D MIND approach may encounter challenges and resistance. In this chapter, we will explore some common obstacles that can arise during the transition to 5D thinking and provide strategies to overcome them. By proactively addressing these challenges, organizations can build a sustainable and resilient corporate culture that embraces the principles of 5D MIND.

4.1 Challenge: Resistance to Change

Resistance to change is one of the most prevalent challenges organizations face when introducing a new framework like 5D MIND. Employees and leaders might be comfortable with the status quo or fear the uncertainty that comes with adopting a new approach.

Overcoming the Challenge:

- **Communicate the purpose:** Clearly communicate the reasons and benefits of embracing 5D MIND. Help employees understand how this shift will improve their work experience, the organization's performance, and its impact on society and the environment.

- **Involve employees in the process:** Encourage open discussions and involve employees in the decision-making process. Give them a voice and let them participate in shaping the implementation of 5D MIND, fostering a sense of ownership and commitment.

- **Provide support and resources:** Offer training and support for employees and leaders to develop the skills needed for 5D thinking. Ensure that they have the resources and tools required to successfully implement the framework.

4.2 Challenge: Existing Hierarchical Structures

Traditional hierarchical structures can hinder collaboration and innovation, which are vital components of 5D thinking.

Overcoming the Challenge:

- **Flatten the hierarchy:** Foster a more flexible organizational structure that encourages collaboration and shared decision-making. Empower employees at all levels to contribute their ideas and insights.

- **Embrace a networked approach:** Create cross-functional teams and project groups to facilitate collaboration across departments. Encourage knowledge-sharing and break down silos.

4.3 Challenge: Short-Term Focus

In the fast-paced business world, short-term thinking can take precedence over long-term vision and sustainability.

Overcoming the Challenge:

- **Set long-term goals:** Establish clear and inspiring long-term goals aligned with the organization's purpose and values. Communicate these goals consistently to keep everyone focused on the bigger picture.

- **Align incentives:** Link incentives and rewards to achieving long-term objectives, fostering a culture that values sustainable practices and visionary thinking.

4.4 Challenge: Lack of Resources

Organizations may face resource constraints when implementing new initiatives, including 5D MIND.

Overcoming the Challenge:

- **Start small:** Begin by piloting 5D MIND initiatives in specific departments or projects. Gradually expand as you demonstrate positive outcomes and secure more resources.

- **Seek partnerships:** Collaborate with like-minded organizations or experts to share resources and knowledge, accelerating the implementation of the 5D MIND framework.

4.5 Challenge: Measurement and Evaluation

Measuring the impact of the 5D MIND approach can be challenging, as some aspects, such as culture and employee engagement, are intangible.

Overcoming the Challenge:

- **Define relevant metrics:** Identify key performance indicators (KPIs) that align with each dimension of 5D MIND. Monitor progress regularly to assess the impact of the framework.

- **Qualitative feedback:** Utilize surveys, interviews, and feedback sessions to gather qualitative data on employee experiences, attitudes, and perceptions of the 5D MIND implementation.

Conclusion:

Transitioning to a 5D MIND approach requires careful consideration of potential challenges and a proactive approach to overcoming them. By addressing resistance to change, adapting hierarchical structures, promoting long-term vision, managing resources effectively, and implementing appropriate measurement methods, organizations can build a sustainable and resilient corporate culture that embraces the principles of 5D thinking. Embrace these strategies to successfully navigate the challenges and unleash the full potential of your organization in the digital age.

Chapter 5
Case Studies of 5D MIND Corporates

In this chapter, we will explore real-life examples of companies that have embraced the 5D MIND framework and witnessed its positive impact on their organizational culture, innovation, and overall success. These case studies highlight how diverse businesses, operating in various industries, have leveraged 5D thinking to thrive in the digital age.

Case Study 1: Patagonia - Dimension of Sustainability

Patagonia, an outdoor clothing and gear company, is a shining example of sustainability and ethical practices. The company has integrated the Dimension of Sustainability into its core values, ensuring that every decision aligns with its commitment to environmental and social responsibility. Patagonia's journey towards 5D MIND began when its founder, Yvon Chouinard, emphasized the need for responsible consumption and environmental stewardship.

Implementation Highlights:

• Patagonia's mission statement explicitly reflects its values: "Build the best product, cause no unnecessary harm, use business to inspire and implement solutions to the environmental crisis."

• The company invests in sustainable materials and manufacturing processes, reducing its environmental footprint while maintaining product quality.

• The Patagonia Worn Wear program promotes a circular economy by encouraging customers to trade in used items for store credits, reducing waste and promoting responsible consumption.

Benefits:

• Enhanced brand reputation: Patagonia's dedication to sustainability has attracted conscious consumers, driving brand loyalty and word-of- mouth marketing.

- Employee motivation: Employees feel proud to work for a company that aligns with their values, leading to higher employee engagement and retention.

- Business resilience: By prioritizing sustainability, Patagonia is better prepared to navigate changing consumer expectations and environmental challenges.

Case Study 2: Google - Dimension of Innovation

Google is synonymous with innovation and has consistently embraced the Dimension of Innovation to maintain its position as a tech leader. From its humble beginnings as a search engine, Google's innovation-focused approach has led to the creation of revolutionary products and services, such as Google Maps, Android, and Google Cloud.

Implementation Highlights:

- Google's "20% Time" policy allows employees to dedicate a portion of their work hours to pursuing personal passion projects, encouraging creativity and innovation.

- The company actively acquires startups and invests in cutting-edge technologies to stay at the forefront of the tech industry.

- Google's culture fosters a growth mindset, where failure is viewed as an opportunity to learn and improve.

Benefits:

- Market leadership: Google's relentless pursuit of innovation has enabled it to dominate multiple sectors within the tech industry.

- Attracting top talent: Google's reputation for innovation attracts some of the brightest minds in the industry, ensuring a talent pool capable of driving ongoing success.

- Diversification: By consistently introducing new products and services, Google diversifies its revenue streams and mitigates risks associated with relying on a single market.

Case Study 3: Salesforce - Dimension of Collaboration

Salesforce, a cloud-based software company, has been highly successful in embracing the Dimension of Collaboration. The company prioritizes a collaborative approach that extends not only to internal teams but also to customers and partners.

Implementation Highlights:

- Salesforce's Customer Success Platform enables seamless collaboration between various teams, such as sales, marketing, and customer service.

- The Trailblazer Community fosters collaboration among Salesforce customers and enthusiasts, facilitating knowledge-sharing and problem- solving.

- The company encourages employees to volunteer and participate in community-driven initiatives, promoting a culture of giving back.

Benefits:

- Enhanced customer experience: Collaboration across departments ensures a holistic approach to customer satisfaction, leading to increased loyalty and retention.

- Innovation through co-creation: Salesforce collaborates with customers to co-create new features and products, ensuring they address real- world needs.

- Employee engagement: A culture of collaboration empowers employees to work together effectively, fostering a sense of camaraderie and shared purpose.

Conclusion:

These case studies demonstrate the transformative power of the 5D MIND framework in diverse organizations. By embracing the dimensions of 5D thinking, these companies have created purpose-driven cultures, encouraged innovation, and achieved sustainable success in the digital age. By drawing inspiration from their experiences, your organization can embark on a similar journey towards a conscious, innovative, and resilient future. Embrace the 5D MIND framework, and let these case studies guide you towards building a better and more prosperous corporate culture.

Chapter 6
The 5D MIND Leader

In the 5D MIND framework, the role of leadership is paramount. A 5D MIND leader is not only skilled in traditional management practices but also embodies the qualities necessary to navigate the complexities of the digital age and foster a conscious and innovative corporate culture. In this chapter, we will explore the qualities and skills required to be an effective 5D MIND leader, providing insights on how to inspire and empower teams, foster a culture of trust, and lead with purpose and integrity.

6.1 Qualities of a 5D MIND Leader:

a) **Self-Awareness:** A 5D MIND leader starts with a deep understanding of themselves. They are emotionally intelligent, aware of their strengths, weaknesses, and biases. By being self-aware, they can lead with authenticity and humility.

b) **Visionary Thinking:** 5D MIND leaders possess a future-oriented mindset, constantly seeking opportunities and anticipating industry trends. They have a clear vision for the organization's long-term success and can effectively communicate it to inspire and align their teams.

c) **Empathy and Compassion:** Empathy is a key quality of a 5D MIND leader. They genuinely care about their team members' well-being and are attentive to their needs, fostering a culture of trust and mutual respect.

d) **Open-Mindedness:** 5D MIND leaders embrace diversity and encourage a culture of open-mindedness. They actively seek out diverse perspectives, recognizing that innovation and creativity thrive in inclusive environments.

e) **Purpose-Driven:** These leaders lead with a higher purpose beyond profit. They prioritize ethical practices and sustainable decision-making, ensuring that the organization contributes positively to society and the environment.

6.2 Skills of a 5D MIND Leader:

a) Communication: Effective communication is a fundamental skill for a 5D MIND leader. They can articulate their vision, provide clear direction, and actively listen to their team members' feedback and ideas.

b) Collaboration: A 5D MIND leader excels at collaboration, fostering teamwork and creating an environment where people feel valued and empowered to contribute their unique skills and perspectives.

c) Innovation: These leaders promote a culture of innovation and are open to experimentation and calculated risk-taking. They encourage their teams to think creatively and challenge the status quo.

d) Emotional Intelligence: Emotional intelligence enables 5D MIND leaders to navigate complex interpersonal dynamics, resolve conflicts, and inspire their teams by understanding and connecting with their emotions.

e) Adaptability: In the dynamic digital age, adaptability is crucial. 5D MIND leaders can pivot quickly in response to changing circumstances, making well-informed decisions in uncertain environments.

6.3 Inspiring and Empowering Teams:

a) Lead by Example: A 5D MIND leader sets the tone by embodying the qualities they wish to see in their teams. They model the values of self-awareness, innovation, collaboration, and sustainability.

b) Delegate and Trust: Empower your team members by delegating tasks and trusting them to make decisions within their areas of expertise. Provide support and guidance, but allow them to take ownership of their work.

c) Encourage Growth: Nurture a culture of continuous learning and development. Support your team members' professional growth and provide opportunities for them to explore new areas and expand their skills.

6.4 Fostering a Culture of Trust:

a) Transparency: Be open and transparent in your communication with your team. Share information, be honest about challenges, and celebrate successes together.

b) Psychological Safety: Create a safe and inclusive environment where team members feel comfortable expressing their ideas and concerns without fear of judgment or reprisal.

c) Recognition and Appreciation: Acknowledge and appreciate your team members' efforts and achievements regularly. Recognizing their contributions fosters a positive and motivated work atmosphere.

6.5 Leading with Purpose and Integrity:

a) Align Actions with Values: Demonstrate consistency between your words and actions. Ensure that your decisions reflect the organization's values and purpose.

b) Ethical Decision-Making: Prioritize ethical practices and responsible decision-making, even when faced with challenging dilemmas. Lead with integrity and accountability.

c) Embrace Sustainability: Incorporate sustainability principles into your leadership approach, making conscious choices that positively impact the environment and society.

Conclusion:

To be an effective 5D MIND leader, it is essential to possess qualities such as self-awareness, visionary thinking, empathy, and open-mindedness, coupled with skills like effective communication, collaboration, and adaptability. By inspiring and empowering teams, fostering a culture of trust, and leading with purpose and integrity, 5D MIND leaders can guide their organizations towards sustainable success in the digital age. Embrace these qualities and skills, and you will be well on your way to becoming a transformative leader who makes a positive impact on your organization and the world.

Chapter 7
Nurturing a Learning Organization

In the fast-paced and ever-changing landscape of the digital age, organizations must become learning organizations to remain competitive and adaptable. Continuous learning is essential for staying ahead of the curve, navigating uncertainty, and embracing disruption as an opportunity for growth. In this chapter, we will explore the importance of continuous learning and provide insights on how to create a learning organization that thrives in the face of uncertainty and disruption.

7.1 The Importance of Continuous Learning:

a) **Adapting to Change:** Continuous learning enables organizations to respond proactively to changes in the market, industry, and technology. By staying informed and updated, they can pivot their strategies and operations swiftly.

b) **Innovation and Creativity:** Learning fosters a culture of innovation and creativity. Employees who are encouraged to learn and explore new ideas are more likely to come up with innovative solutions to challenges.

c) **Talent Development and Retention:** A learning organization attracts and retains top talent. Employees are more likely to stay with a company that invests in their growth and provides opportunities for skill development.

d) **Resilience and Agility:** In the face of uncertainty and disruption, a learning organization can adapt quickly and make informed decisions. Continuous learning builds resilience and agility in times of change.

7.2 Building a Learning Organization:

a) **Emphasize a Growth Mindset:** Promote a growth mindset at all levels of the organization. Encourage employees to view challenges as opportunities to learn and grow, rather than obstacles.

b) **Provide Learning Opportunities:** Offer various learning opportunities, including workshops, webinars, conferences, and online courses. Tailor these opportunities to meet the specific needs and interests of employees.

c) Support Knowledge-Sharing: Encourage knowledge-sharing among employees. Create platforms and forums where employees can exchange ideas, best practices, and lessons learned.

d) Foster a Culture of Curiosity: Cultivate a culture where curiosity and questioning are encouraged. Employees should feel empowered to explore new concepts and challenge existing assumptions.

e) Lead by Example: Leaders should model continuous learning and demonstrate their commitment to personal and professional growth. When leaders prioritize learning, it sets the tone for the entire organization.

7.3 Creating Learning Opportunities:

a) Training and Development Programs: Invest in comprehensive training and development programs that cater to different job roles and skill levels within the organization.

b) Learning Partnerships: Collaborate with external training providers, universities, or industry experts to offer specialized training and learning experiences.

c) Mentorship and Coaching: Establish mentorship and coaching programs to provide personalized guidance and support for employees' growth and development.

d) Innovation Labs and Hackathons: Organize innovation labs and hackathons where employees can experiment with new ideas and technologies, fostering a culture of innovation.

e) Learning Budgets: Allocate budgets for employees to access external courses or attend conferences related to their field of interest or professional development.

7.4 Measuring Learning Outcomes:

a) Assessing Individual Growth: Track individual employees' learning progress and skill development to identify areas of improvement and support their professional growth.

b) Impact on Organizational Performance: Measure how learning initiatives impact the organization's performance, innovation, and agility.

c) Employee Feedback: Gather feedback from employees about the effectiveness of learning programs and identify areas for improvement.

Conclusion:

Nurturing a learning organization is crucial for thriving in the face of uncertainty and disruption. Continuous learning empowers employees, enhances innovation, and fosters resilience and adaptability. By emphasizing a growth mindset, providing learning opportunities, fostering a culture of curiosity, and measuring learning outcomes, organizations can create an environment where learning becomes an integral part of their DNA. Embrace continuous learning as a core value, and your organization will be better equipped to tackle challenges, embrace change, and excel in the dynamic digital age.